THE SCHOOLS HISTORY PROJECT
S·H·P
OFFICIAL TEXT

DISCOVERING THE PAST FOR GCSE

RUSSIA & THE USSR 1905–1941

a study in depth

TERRY FIEHN

Series Editor: Colin Shephard

Hodder Murray
www.hoddereducation.co.uk

© Terry Fiehn 1996

First published in 1996
by John Murray (Publishers) Ltd, a member of the Hodder Headline Group
338 Euston Road
London NW1 3BH

Reprinted 1998, 1999, 2001, 2002 (twice), 2003 (twice), 2004 , 2005 , 2006

Layouts by Eric Drewery
Artwork by Jeff Edwards, Mike Humphries, Linden Artists,
Chris Mutter and Steve Smith
Typeset in 10½/12 pt Walbaum Book by Anneset, Weston-
super-Mare
Printed and bound in Dubai by Oriental Press
A catalogue entry for this title is available from the British
Library

ISBN-10:0-7195-5255-9
ISBN-13:978 0 719 55255 7
Teachers' Resource Book ISBN 0-7195-5256-7

Contents

CONTENTS

The Schools History Project

This project was set up by the Schools Council in 1972. Its main aim was to suggest suitable objectives for history teachers, and to promote the use of appropriate materials and teaching methods for their realisation. This involved a reconsideration of the nature of history and its relevance in secondary schools, the design of a syllabus framework which shows the uses of history in the education of adolescents, and the setting up of appropriate examinations.

Since 1978 the project has been based at Trinity and All Saints' College, Leeds. It is now self-funding and with the advent of the National Curriculum it has expanded its publications to provide courses for Key Stage 3, and for a range of GCSE and A level syllabuses. The project provides INSET for all aspects of National Curriculum, GCSE and A level history, and also publishes *Discoveries*, a twice-yearly journal for history teachers.

Enquiries about the *Discovering the Past* series should be addressed to the publishers, John Murray.

Series consultants
Terry Fiehn
Tim Lomas
Martin and Jenny Tucker

Note: The wording and sentence structure of some written sources have been adapted and simplified to make them accessible to all pupils, while faithfully preserving the sense of the original.

Words printed in SMALL CAPITALS are defined in the Glossary on page 128.

Acknowledgements

Cover photos: *left* Russian poster showing men and women working as equals. The caption reads: 'We destroyed the enemies with weapons. We'll earn our bread with labour – comrades roll up your sleeves for work.'; *right* Propaganda poster celebrating Stalin's second Five-Year Plan. Both courtesy of David King.

All photos are reproduced courtesy of David King except for the following:

p.4 *c* SCR Photo Library, *r* State Archive of Film and Photographic Documents, St. Petersburg; **p.8** *b* SCR Photo Library; **p.9** *t* State Archive of Film and Photographic Documents, St. Petersburg, *b* The Mansell Collection; **p.20** *b* Novosti (London); **p.34** *t* Novosti (London); **p.55** By permission of The British Library; **p.61** *article* © Times Newspapers Limited, 1994, *r* Illustrator Phil Green/The Sunday Times, London; **p.65** Novosti (London); **p.66** from B. Efimov, *Caricatures*, 1924; **p.67** *r* Novosti (London); **p.98** *t* Novosti (London); **p.101** *b* Russian State Archive of Film and Photographic Documents, Krasnogorsk; **p.107** B.T. Batsford Ltd; **p.111** Alexander Chunosov/Network; **p.120** *bl* Internationaal Instituut voor Sociale Geschiedenis, Amsterdam; **p.123** International Film Foundation, New York; **p.125** © Archives SNARK/Edimedia, Paris.

(*t* = top, *b* = bottom, *r* = right, *l* = left, *c* = centre)

Every effort has been made to trace all the copyright holders, but if any have been inadvertently overlooked the publishers will be pleased to make the necessary arrangement at the first opportunity.

TSARIST RUSSIA: HOW WELL DID THE TSAR GOVERN RUSSIA?

chapter 1

WAS RUSSIA WELL GOVERNED IN 1900?

Why was Russia so difficult to govern?

AT THE BEGINNING of the twentieth century, Russia was a vast empire spanning two continents – Europe and Asia. From west to east it stretched over 4,000 miles, from north to south some 2,000 miles. The USA could fit into Russia two and a half times over and Britain nearly 100 times. When it was night on one side of the empire, it was day on the other.

Communications were difficult. There were few paved roads. Outside the main cities, most of the roads were hard-packed earth, which would turn to mud in heavy rain. In the villages and small towns in spring and autumn, people had to walk on platforms or boards to avoid sinking in the mud, which could suck off their boots. In the winter, the frozen ruts would bounce people along as they travelled in their horse-drawn sleds. Travel by road was slow at the best of times and roads often became impassable.

For longer journeys, people used the rivers or the railways. Many of the major cities were sited along the rivers. Passenger steamboats plied regularly up and down the main routes, such as the River Volga. In the winter, the rivers iced over and sleds could be used.

Railways were the most comfortable form of travel. There had been an enormous growth in railways in the 1890s, but by 1900 Russia had only as many miles of track as Britain. Most of these were in European Russia. The only line of communication across the vast eastern expanse was the Trans-Siberian railway, which was opened in 1904. It took more than a week on the Trans-Siberian Express to travel from Moscow in the west to Vladivostok on the Pacific coast.

The Russian Empire covered about one-sixth of the world's total land, with a vast range of landscapes. The northern part of Russia, the tundra, is frozen for most of the year. South of the tundra is the taiga, which consists of miles and miles of impenetrable forests, and then the Russian Steppes, a vast area of grassland. In the far south lies the desert, where nomads used camels for their journeys to far-flung settlements.

Much of this land was very beautiful and dramatic, but little of it could be used for farming. The main agricultural areas were in European Russia, where most of the people lived. The Black Earth region was the most fertile. Beyond the Ural Mountains, Russia was a wild place, with frontier settlements very like the old Wild West of America.

SOURCE 1   A man and his son on a street in a provincial Russian town

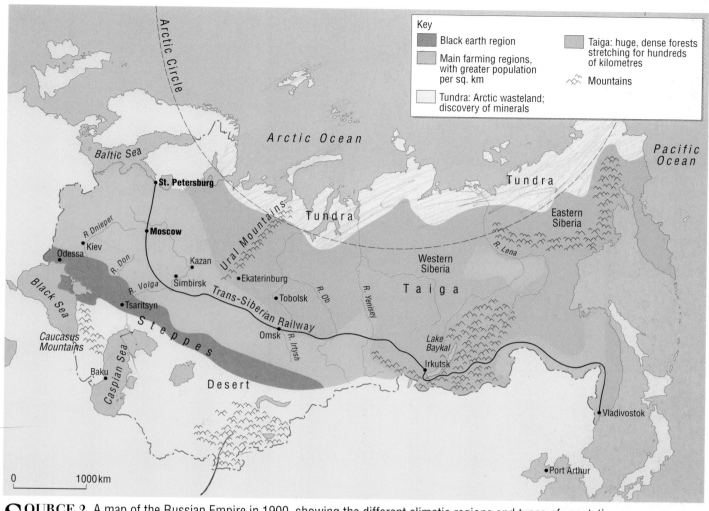

SOURCE 2 A map of the Russian Empire in 1900, showing the different climatic regions and types of vegetation

SOURCE 3 Peasant women pulling boats on the Volga River

1. How do you think that each of the following helps explain why Russia was difficult to govern:

- size
- climate
- communications?

Who were the Russians?

The Empire contained around 130 million people, the vast majority of whom lived in European Russia, west of the Ural Mountains. But less than half of the population were Russians. The rest belonged to peoples who had been conquered by the Russians. Many of them did not speak Russian and most were illiterate.

1. Why did so many people live in the European part of Russia?

Nationality	Millions
Russian	55.6
Ukrainian	22.4
White Russian	5.8
Polish	7.9
Jewish	5.0
Kirghiz	4.0
Tartar	3.4
German	1.8
Latvian	1.4
Bashkir	1.3
Lithuanian	1.2
Armenian	1.2
Romanian/Moldavian	1.1
Estonian	1.0
Georgian	0.8
Turkmenian	0.3

SOURCE 4 The major nationalities in Russia by mother tongue in 1897

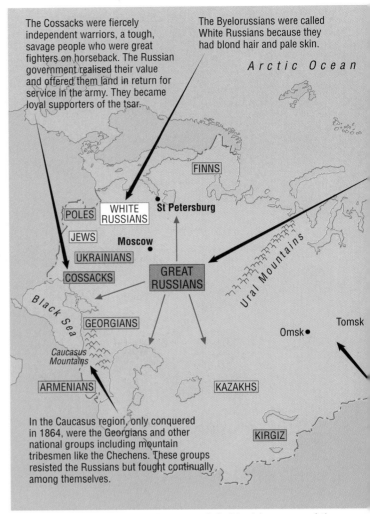

The Cossacks were fiercely independent warriors, a tough, savage people who were great fighters on horseback. The Russian government realised their value and offered them land in return for service in the army. They became loyal supporters of the tsar.

The Byelorussians were called White Russians because they had blond hair and pale skin.

Arctic Ocean

FINNS

POLES | WHITE RUSSIANS | St Petersburg

JEWS | Moscow

UKRAINIANS

COSSACKS | GREAT RUSSIANS | *Ural Mountains*

Black Sea | GEORGIANS | Omsk | Tomsk

Caucasus Mountains

ARMENIANS | KAZAKHS

In the Caucasus region, only conquered in 1864, were the Georgians and other national groups including mountain tribesmen like the Chechens. These groups resisted the Russians but fought continually among themselves.

KIRGIZ

SOURCE 5 Map showing areas inhabited by some of the different nationalities

SOURCE 6 Gurians from the Caucasus

SOURCE 7 Evenki people from Siberia

SOURCE 8 Muscovites waiting at a tram stop

he Great Russians, a mixture of Slavs and Vikings, were characterised as a
elancholy, gloomy people, given to outbursts of emotion. This was put
own to the hard climate, long dark nights and long periods of inactivity.
he Russians were convinced that they were special. They thought that the
ussian customs and religion were superior to those of their neighbours.
om the fifteenth century onwards, they began to conquer the peoples
ound them one by one.

Russian empire grew up with Moscow at its centre. Here the tsars, the
lers of Russia, lived. In the seventeenth century, Peter the Great moved the
pital to St Petersburg and the empire was extended across the Ural
ountains into Asia. But it was not until the end of the nineteenth century that
any of the areas in the south and in the east came under Russian control.

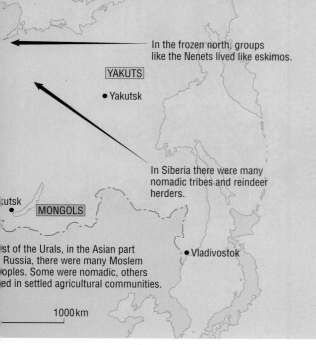

In the frozen north, groups
like the Nenets lived like eskimos.

YAKUTS

• Yakutsk

In Siberia there were many
nomadic tribes and reindeer
herders.

kutsk
• MONGOLS

• Vladivostok

st of the Urals, in the Asian part
Russia, there were many Moslem
oples. Some were nomadic, others
ed in settled agricultural communities.

1000 km

Russification

Some of the national groups were deeply resentful of
Russian control. They particularly resented the
policy of 'Russification' – making non-Russians
speak Russian, wear Russian clothes and follow
Russian customs – which they saw as an attack on
their way of life.

Russian officials were brought in to run the
government of non-Russian areas of the Empire,
such as Finland, Poland and Latvia. The Russian
language had to be used in schools, in law courts
and in local government. In Poland it was forbidden
to teach children in Polish. Russians were also given
the important jobs in non-Russian areas.

2. Draw a bar chart showing the size of the seven
   largest groups in Russia.
3. What do Sources 1, 3 and 5–9 suggest about
   differences in the lives of the people in different
   parts of Russia? Choose three photographs to
   illustrate your points.
4. Do you think the existence of the different
   national groups would make it easier or harder to
   govern Russia? Think about:

   ■ different languages and ways of life
   ■ attitudes towards the Russians and
     Russification
   ■ divisions between national groups who
     disliked each other.

SOURCE 9   Jews from Bokhara in central Asia

What was life like in Russia in 1900?

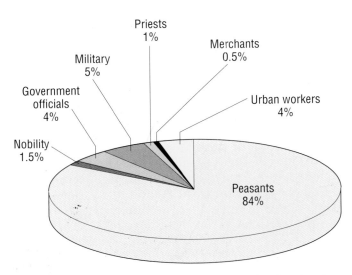

Priests
1%

Merchants
0.5%

Military
5%

Government
officials
4%

Urban workers
4%

Nobility
1.5%

Peasants
84%

SOURCE 1 A breakdown of Russian society by class in 1900

1. What do Sources 1 and 2 tell you about Russian society?
2. Do you think the cartoonist who drew Source 2 approved of the way Russian society was organised? Explain your answer.

The peasants

AT THE BEGINNING of the twentieth century, four out of every five people in Russia were peasants. For most of them, life was hard. Their main food was grain made into rye bread or porridge, and cabbage soup. Fish was common but meat was rare. On religious days and at festivals delicacies such as pies and pancakes were eaten. Tea, beer and vodka were the most popular drinks.

When the harvests were good there was food to go around. But when the harvests were bad there was starvation and disease: 400,000 people died in 1891 when crop failure coupled with cholera hit the countryside. The average life expectancy was less than 40 years. There were regular epidemics of typhus and diphtheria, and syphilis was widespread. It was a life of poverty, squalor and, often, drunkenness.

The peasants used the backward strip method of farming – each family had 20 to 30 or more narrow strips scattered around the village. They used wooden ploughs and had few animals or tools, so the work was backbreaking physical labour. Most families only produced enough food for themselves. Some peasants earned extra money by making clothes, furniture or articles to sell in the towns.

We rule you.

We govern you.

We fool you.

We shoot you.

We eat instead of you.

We work for you. We feed you.

SOURCE 2 A cartoon showing Russian society, drawn in about 1900

But the main problem was land. There was simply not enough to go round. Until 1861, the majority of peasants had been SERFS, owned by their masters. In 1861, they had been freed and were allocated a share of land which they could buy with money loaned by the government. But they had to pay off the loans over many years. Moreover, the amount of land they got was often barely enough to survive on, let alone pay off loans. As a result, many peasants got into crushing debt.

The peasants were angry that the landowners, the nobles, had kept so much of the land after 1861 and still had large estates. Many had to work on the nobles' estates to earn extra money. Most peasants simply wanted enough of their own land to farm. The situation was getting worse by 1900. The population had increased by 50 per cent between 1860 and 1897 and was still growing fast. More and more peasants were competing for the land available.

SOURCE 3 Peasants in a village near Nizhny-Novogorod, 1891–92

SOURCE 4 A peasant mother and her children sleeping in a hut

Typically, Russian peasants wore coarse woollen shirts and trousers and peaked caps. Their loose trousers were tucked into leather boots if they were well off. The poorest wore sandals made of tree bark. Women wore cotton blouses, often coloured, skirts, and scarves on their heads. Men and women wore kaftan coats tied at the waist.

SOURCE 6 A description of peasants' homes by an English visitor

SOURCE 5 Peasants at a village meal (see Source 3)

66 The village consists of one street, containing about 35 cottages, and lined with birch trees. The cottages are built of wood and are unpainted . . . You mount a wooden staircase or ladder, push open a door, and find yourself in the upper or main floor of the cottage, the ground floor being mainly used for storage purposes. A big brick stove is in the main room, and on this stove the older people and children sleep in winter. There is a rough table and a few chairs, a bed and in the middle of the room a child's cot suspended from the ceiling. 99

3. What can you see in Sources 3, 4 and 5 to suggest that the peasants were poor?
4. In what ways does Source 6 agree with the evidence of the photographs?
5. Give two reasons why the peasants were so poor.
6. Why was the issue of land so important to the peasants?
7. What would your main complaints be if you were a peasant? Make a list under the following headings: food, health, work, money, land.

The nobility

Although the nobles made up just over one per cent of the population, they owned almost a quarter of all the land.

Some were extremely rich, with large country estates, which they employed people to run. They would often also have another home in St Petersburg or Moscow, or both, and would spend a good part of the year enjoying the ballet, the theatre and a round of social events in 'society'.

SOURCE 7   The ball of the coloured wigs at Countess Yelisaveta Shuvalova's palace in St Petersburg

The middle classes

Around 1900, with the development of industry, a new class of people was growing in Russia: bankers, merchants and rich capitalists who owned the industrial works. St Petersburg and Moscow were the main centres of commerce and of the textile industry. The link between rich businessmen and the government in Russia was very strong; the government gave them big contracts and loans.

Life for the rich middle classes was very good. In Moscow there were restaurants, cocktail bars and smart hotels. Here they could eat good Russian food – caviar, sturgeon, cold salmon and borsch (beetroot and meat soup served with cream) – and drink champagne. They could go to the much-loved ballet, to concerts or the theatre. They had large houses which were lavishly decorated, with beautiful furniture.

■ ACTIVITY

Compare the lives of the rich and poor in Russia at the beginning of the twentieth century. Divide a page into two columns headed rich and poor.

a) Use the evidence – the photographs and the written sources – to compare their clothes, food, work, housing, entertainment, and other aspects of their lives.

b) Write several sentences to answer this question: 'How large was the gap between rich and poor in Russia at the beginning of the twentieth century?'

SOURCE 8   A painting of a middle-class family being entertained by a street musician

S OURCE 9   A soup kitchen for the unemployed before 1914

S OURCE 10   From *The Story of My Life*, by Father Gapon, written in 1905. Gapon was a priest who organised a trade union to help workers

❝ *They receive miserable wages, and generally live in an overcrowded state, very commonly in special lodging houses. A woman takes several rooms in her own name, subletting each one; and it is common to see ten or more persons living in one room and four sleeping in a bed.*

The normal working day is eleven and a half hours of work, exclusive of meal times. But . . . manufacturers have received permission to work overtime, so that the average day is longer than that nominally allowed by law – fifteen or sixteen hours. I often watched the crowds of poorly clad and emaciated figures of men and girls returning from the mills . . . Why do they agree to work overtime? They have to do so because they are paid by the piece and the rate is very low. ❞

S OURCE 11   A report from the journal of the Moscow municipal corporation in 1902 on tenement buildings in the city

❝ *The apartment has a terrible appearance, the plaster is crumbling, there are holes in the walls, stopped up with rags. It is dirty. The stove has collapsed. Legions of cockroaches and bugs. No double window frames and so it is piercingly cold. The lavatory is so dilapidated that it is dangerous to enter and children are not allowed in. All apartments in the house are similar.* ❞

The workers

Life in the back streets of St Petersburg, Moscow and other Russian cities was very different for the men and women who worked in the new industries. They lived in cheap wooden lodging houses or large tenement buildings, ate cheap black bread, cabbage soup and buckwheat porridge – and drank vodka.

In industrial centres away from the cities, workers often lived in barracks next to the factory. Inside, dark corridors led to dormitories for up to 30 workers, or minute rooms sleeping several families. Spaces between them were divided off by flimsy partitions or sheets, giving almost no privacy. Illness, smells, arguments, sex – nothing could be hidden. Many factories kept going 24 hours a day, and the same beds were occupied by two workers in turn, one on the day shift and one on the night shift.

Many of the workers were young male peasants who had been forced off the land. A large number of women workers were employed in the textile factories in Moscow and St Petersburg.

1. Which sources are most useful to historians – the photographs, Sources 9 and 12, or the written sources (10 and 11)?
2. What would your main grievances be if you were a worker?

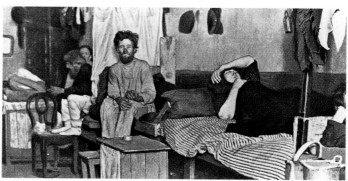

S OURCE 12   A photograph showing the inside of a lodging house

How was Russia governed in 1900?

SOURCE 1 Tsar Nicholas II and Tsarina Alexandra in full regalia

SOURCE 2 An extract from an open letter from Leo Tolstoy, the famous novelist, to the Tsar in 1902

"A third of the whole of Russia lives under reinforced surveillance . . . The army of the police, regular and secret, is continually growing in numbers. The prisons and penal colonies are overcrowded with thousands of convicts and political prisoners, among whom industrial workers are now included . . .

The censorship has reached a level not known since the 1840s . . .

In all cities and industrial centres, soldiers are employed and equipped with live ammunition to be sent out against the people.

. . . and the peasants, all 100,000,000 of them, are getting poorer every year . . . Famine has become a normal phenomenon. Normal likewise is the discontent of all classes of society with the government."

NICHOLAS II, of the Romanov dynasty, came to the throne in 1894. He was an AUTOCRAT. This means that he had complete and absolute power. He was not elected. He believed that he had a divine right to rule – that is, that he had been chosen by God. He could do what he liked without consulting anyone. He had the power of life and death over his subjects.

To help him rule, he had a council of ministers who ran the various government departments. But they all reported to the Tsar, who made the important decisions.

Because Russia was such a large country to run, there were thousands of civil servants, from top officials down to tax collectors and customs officers. Getting things done was a painfully slow business. The civil servants carried out the orders passed down to them. However, since the wages of the people at the bottom were very low, there was a good deal of bribery and corruption.

There was no parliament to represent the views of the people, and there was no way for people to get their views heard. Newspapers and books were CENSORED: they had to be sent to the government for approval before they could be printed. Opposition was not tolerated, and the Okhrana, or secret police, dealt with anyone who criticised the government. The secret police had spies and agents everywhere. DISSIDENTS soon found themselves in jail or exiled to Siberia.

If there were strikes, protests or riots, which often took place in times of famine, then soldiers, particularly the much-feared Cossacks, would be used to restore order. They stopped any demonstrations with great brutality.

1. Explain in your own words the meaning of the word 'autocrat'.
2. What impression of the Tsar and his wife was Source 1 designed to put across?

SOURCE 3 Political prisoners, including the revolutionary Marie Spirodonova (left; see page 15)

SOURCE 4   From *Russia as it Really Is*, written in 1904 by Carl Joubert, a French doctor. Here he describes some of the prisoners he examined who were going to Siberia

❝■ *A young man, aged twenty, a student from Kazan, stated that he had committed no crime: but he was found reading a certain book in which the censor's name did not figure on the title page, was arrested by the secret police, and sent for five years hard labour . . . I examined him and found him in the second stage of consumption. His troubles would soon be over.*

■ *A girl, aged nineteen, from Taganrog, stated that she was found in the house of a revolutionary. The revolutionary got away before arrest, but she was taken, though absolutely innocent, as a substitute. No trial. Twenty years' [sentence] . . . Examined her and found that she was suffering from cancer of the breast. Nothing had been done for her.*

■ *A woman, aged 27, from the city of Moscow, wife of a lawyer. Her husband, in the same prison, was sentenced to ten years for being in possession of certain books. Health: advanced pregnancy.*

Such were a few of the cases that came to my notice . . . It is not therefore surprising that a large number of them never reach their destinations. **❞**

The Orthodox Church

The Orthodox Church – a branch of Christianity – was very important in Russia. In most houses there were holy pictures or icons on the walls. The Orthodox Church was surrounded by mysticism and superstition. Holy men, or STARTSY (one STARETS) were held in special regard. However, there was a great gap between the poor parish priests on one side and the rich bishops and higher clergy on the other.

The Orthodox Church was closely linked to the Tsar and supported his way of ruling. It taught that the Tsar was the head of the country and the head of the Church – in other words, that he was God's chosen representative on earth. This was why many peasants and workers thought of the Tsar as the 'little father', their special protector. But this image was to be shattered in the early part of the new century.

3. Do Sources 2–4 suggest that the system of governing Russia was working well? Explain your answer.
4. What do each of the cases in Source 4 tell us about the Tsar's method of keeping control?
5. How do you think the Orthodox Church helped to keep the Tsar in power?
6. What aspects of the way that Russia was governed do you think made people most angry?

■ ACTIVITY

You are a Russian noble who believes that there is a lot wrong with Russia in the year 1903. You have spent some time in Moscow and St Petersburg and have toured around many villages. Write a letter to the Tsar telling him what is wrong and why changes need to be made. Mention:

■ the poverty of the peasants and the land problem
■ the living and working conditions of the industrial workers
■ corruption in government
■ censorship of the press
■ the violence used to deal with protesters
■ the lack of opportunity for people to have their views heard.

You could begin like this:

5 June 1903

Sire,
Your most loyal and obedient servant wishes to draw to your attention the grievous situation and serious problems existing in some parts of Russia today. I know that, were you fully aware of these, you would take steps to improve matters. I have recently completed a tour of . . .

Was the Tsar fit to rule Russia?

THE SYSTEM OF government in Russia meant that a lot depended on the man at the centre – the Tsar. He had to be a strong person, capable of making hard decisions and controlling his ministers. Was Nicholas II up to the job?

Tsar Nicholas II

There is no doubt that Nicholas was a kind, well-meaning person, with a deep affection for his family. He was devoted to his wife, Alexandra, his son, Alexis, and his four daughters, Tatiana, Olga, Maria and Anastasia. Family photographs were in every room of the palace, including the lavatory. Nicholas would sooner spend time with his family than deal with governmental matters.

Although kind to those around him and deeply religious, Nicholas could also be cruel and merciless. He would not stand for opposition. His answer was always the same – violence. He praised regiments who put down disorder and hanged the people involved. He was particularly anti-Jewish and encouraged POGROMS (attacks) against Jewish settlements.

Nicholas believed wholeheartedly in autocracy. He thought that democracy with elections and parliaments would lead to the collapse of Russia.

It does seem that he genuinely wanted to bring happiness and prosperity to his people. Unfortunately, Nicholas knew very little about the people. He did not visit factories or villages, or go on tours. His information about what was going on came from a small number of people, who were quite happy to protect him from the realities of life in Russia.

His wife: Alexandra

The Tsarina Alexandra, Nicholas's wife, had a very different type of personality. Although shy, she was strong willed and obstinate.

She was also very religious. She believed that the

SOURCE 1 A photograph of the Tsar with his wife Alexandra and their children

Tsar had been appointed by God and that it was her duty to support him.

Alexandra was clearly very much in love with Nicholas. In the evenings, she demanded that he spend time with the family. She encouraged the Tsar to withdraw from public events to a private family world.

The Tsarina had a great influence on the Tsar. She was determined that Nicholas should not share power with the people. She felt Nicholas should keep all his autocratic powers, given to him by God, to pass on to their son.

1. How might Alexandra have had a harmful influence on her husband in his role as leader?

What did his contemporaries say?

SOURCE 2   Written by Kerensky, the leader of the government which took over from the Tsar in 1917, in his memoirs, *Crucifixion of Liberty*, in 1934

❝ *The daily work of a monarch he found intolerably boring. He could not stand listening long or seriously to ministers' reports, or reading them.* ❞

SOURCE 3   Said by an unknown cabinet minister

❝ *Nicholas II was not fit to run a village post office.* ❞

SOURCE 4   Written by Leon Trotsky, one of the leaders of the revolutionaries who opposed the Tsar, in 1932

❝ *His ancestors did not pass on to him one quality which would have made him capable of governing an empire.* ❞

SOURCE 5   From the diary of the Tsar's sister, the Grand Duchess Olga

❝ *He kept saying . . . that he was wholly unfit to reign . . . And yet Nicky's unfitness was by no means his fault. He had intelligence, he had faith and courage and he was wholly ignorant about governmental matters. Nicky had been trained as a soldier. He should have been taught statesmanship, and he was not.* ❞

SOURCE 6   By Grand Duke Alexander Mikhailovich

❝ *He never had an opinion of his own . . . always agreeing with the judgement of the last person he spoke to.* ❞

SOURCE 7   By Sergei Witte, chief minister under Nicholas, in his memoirs. Even though he disliked the Tsar, he said this of Nicholas

❝ *He has a quick mind and learns easily. In this respect he is far superior to his father.* ❞

2. What did Nicholas's contemporaries (people who lived at the same time) think of him as a ruler (Sources 2–7)?

3. a) Are there any reasons why some of these people might want to run Nicholas down and make him out to be worse than he was?

b) Which of these sources would you trust most? Why?

c) Which would you trust least? Why?

What do historians say?

SOURCE 8 From *Nicholas II, Emperor of All the Russias*, by Dominic Lieven, 1994

66 *Nicholas II was not a stupid man . . . His problem was that he could understand many points of view and wavered between them. The problems Russia faced were very great . . . Nicholas II loved his country and served it loyally and to the best of his ability. He had not sought power and his personality meant that he was not very good at exercising it. He was very kind, sensitive, generous . . . [The situation] would probably have destroyed any man who sat on the throne.* 99

SOURCE 9 From *Russia in the Age of Modernisation and Revolution* by H. Rogger, 1983

66 *Even more poorly prepared than his father for the burdens of kingship, Nicholas had no knowledge of the world of men, of politics or government to help him make the weighty decisions that in the Russian system the Tsar alone must make.* 99

1. Read the opinions of the historians in Sources 8 and 9.
a) Which historian's opinion is supported by most contemporary views?
b) Find one contemporary view to support each of the historians.

■ ACTIVITY

Work in pairs or groups.

1. Choose three qualities which you think a strong leader for Tsarist Russia should have.
2. How does Nicholas measure up against each of these?
3. Read through all the sources on pages 12–14 and decide which of these statements sums up Nicholas best:

a) *He was useless as a Tsar. He was stupid, incompetent and totally unfit for the role of a powerful leader.*

c) *He was an intelligent man, but he had not been prepared for the job of Tsar and really was not up to it.*

b) *He was not as bad as some people made him out to be, but he was not the right man for the job. He was unsuited for it.*

d) *It was an impossible job with all the problems in Russia at this time. Any person would have had great difficulty being Tsar in this period.*

4. Use these statements, or a combination of them, to help you write your own opinion about Nicholas. Use the sources to support your views.

2 HOW DID THE TSAR SURVIVE THE 1905 REVOLUTION?

W*ho opposed the Tsar?*

THERE WERE MANY people in Russia who did not like the way the Tsar governed the Empire. They believed there were better ways of running the country and improving the living conditions of the people. By the early 1900s, a number of groups had emerged who opposed the Tsar.

Socialist Revolutionaries

Formed in 1901, the SOCIALIST REVOLUTIONARIES believed in a general revolutionary movement which would unite all the people who were suffering under the Tsar. They thought the peasants would bring about revolution in Russia.

SOCIALIST REVOLUTIONARIES

Aims
■ To get rid of the Tsar and his government.
■ To give all the land to the peasants to farm collectively in communes – so forming thousands of small peasant communities.

Support
■ Mainly appealed to the peasants, who supported the party which wanted to give them the land. Sometimes called the 'Peasants' Party'.

Tactics
■ Propaganda to encourage revolution.
■ Violent acts (terrorism) to bring about the collapse of the government. Responsible for the deaths of several important government officials.

S**OURCE 1** The cover of the magazine *Raven* (1906) showing tsarist ministers being blown up

Marie Spirodonova

Marie Spirodonova came from a well-to-do family. In 1906 she was a 19-year-old student in Tambov and was deeply affected by the suffering of the peasants around her. She became a Socialist Revolutionary and decided to kill the cruel governor of Tambov. He tortured peasants who could not pay their taxes and used his Cossacks to mistreat them. She walked up to him at a railway station and shot him in the heart.

The Cossacks beat her and threw her naked into a cold cell. When she would not give them the names of accomplices, they pulled out her hair and burnt her all over with cigarettes. For two nights she was passed around the Cossacks. She was sentenced to death but this was changed to life imprisonment in Siberia. She was freed by the 1917 revolution.

Social Democrats

The Social Democratic Party, founded in 1895, followed the teachings of Karl Marx. They believed a revolution would be started by the workers concentrated in large cities.

SOCIAL DEMOCRATS

Aims
- To overthrow the Tsar.
- To create a SOCIALIST state.

Support
- Workers in cities and large towns.
- Students.

Tactics
In 1903, the Social Democrats split over the tactics they thought would bring about revolution. One group became known as the MENSHEVIKS and the other as the BOLSHEVIKS.

Mensheviks believed the party should be a mass organisation which all workers could join. This mass party would grow until it eventually took power. It would work with other groups like trade unions to improve wages and working conditions.

Bolsheviks believed in a small, secret, tightly disciplined party of professional revolutionaries who would seize power when the time was right. They thought that a large party could always be infiltrated by police spies. They planned revolutionary cells of three or four people who would get into factories to organise strikes and demonstrations.

Lenin – real name Vladimir Ilyich Ulyanov

Vladimir Ulyanov was born in Simbirsk in 1870, the son of a school inspector. He was deeply affected by the execution of his revolutionary brother, who had been involved in the assassination of Alexander II. He vowed that he would fight the injustice of Tsarism. He went to

SOURCE 2 A photograph of Lenin taken in around 1900

university to study law, but was expelled because he took part in demonstrations. Later he changed his name to Lenin.

Lenin became more involved with Marxism, writing pamphlets and supporting strikes, and in 1894 formed a MARXIST group. His activities soon led to his arrest and exile to Siberia. Here he married Nadezhda Krupskaya, a fellow revolutionary.

On their release in 1900, Lenin and Nadezhda went abroad to work with the new Social Democratic Party in exile. They came to London, where Lenin helped edit the Party newspaper, *Iskra* ('The Spark'). He developed his ideas about revolution, which caused the split of the Social Democratic Party. The Bolsheviks followed his idea for a small, secret, highly disciplined party, which would seize power in the name of the workers. Lenin remained outside Russia, organising the Bolshevik Party, until the revolution broke out in 1917.

SOURCE 3 Photograph of Trotsky in a prison cell after his arrest in 1905

Trotsky – real name Lev Bronstein

Lev Bronstein was born in 1879 in the Ukraine, the son of a rich Jewish peasant. Angry at the mistreatment of the Jews, he joined a Marxist discussion group at the age of 16 and fell in love with Alexandra Sokolovska, who was the leader of the group. They were arrested for writing revolutionary pamphlets and leading strikes. Married in a Moscow prison, they were exiled to Siberia.

In 1902, his wife helped him escape abroad, using a false passport, which he signed in the name of Trotsky (it was the name of a prison warder). In Paris, he met a young Russian art student called Natalia Sedova. He lived with her for the rest of his life, and they had two sons, although he always kept on good terms with his first wife and family. He went to London to work with Lenin and his wife Krupskaya. They called him 'the Pen' because he was such a good writer. But at the Social Democratic conference in 1903, he sided with the Mensheviks.

In February 1905, he returned from exile to join in the revolution, becoming Menshevik chairman of the St Petersburg SOVIET in October. When the revolution collapsed, Trotsky was arrested and sent back to Siberia. But he escaped on the way and went to America.

Liberals

The liberal middle classes thought it was time the people had an opportunity to run the country though a parliament. In 1905, the liberals formed the Constitutional Democratic Party, the Cadets.

LIBERALS

Aims
- Free elections and a parliament to run the country.
- The Tsar to be a constitutional monarch like the one in England.
- Civil rights – freedom of speech, worship and conscience.

Support
- The middle and educated classes – teachers, doctors, lawyers, some industrialists.
- Some members of the gentry.

Tactics
- Meetings, speeches, discussions, publishing articles and books calling for change.

■ TASK

Look at the statements below. Match each one to the person you think would have said it, and say which opposition group you think they might have supported.

- Railwayman
- Peasant farmer
- Student
- Doctor
- Jewish teacher
- Factory worker

It is time the people had a say in the running of the country. There should be a parliament which is freely elected by all men.

The only way to bring down this evil government is to use terrorism against the Tsar and his officials.

The workers have suffered for too long. We must overthrow the Tsar and build a state where people work co-operatively and share the fruits of their labour.

The capitalists squeeze as much work out of the working people as they can for the least amount of wages while they live well with lovely houses, clothes and food.

The land should be taken from the rich landlords and given to the people who work on it.

People should have equal civil rights, including the freedom to speak and write without censorship. They should have an equal chance to get jobs and set up businesses.

Discussion point
Do you think terrorism is ever justified in trying to change the way a country is governed?

Why did Russia explode in revolution in 1905?

IN 1905 RUSSIA reached boiling point and revolution broke out. For a year, the Tsar was unable to control large areas of Russia. How did this come about? People had been dissatisfied with the government for a long time but it needed other factors to push Russia into open revolution.

Economic problems

We have already seen that the living and working conditions for peasants and workers were very bad. But the government made matters worse by its own policies.

Russia needed to develop its industries in order to change from a backward agricultural country into a modern industrialised one, and remain an important military power. So the government invested an enormous amount of money in improving Russia's industries. Although money was borrowed from other countries, the main source was the Russian people.

The peasants had to pay heavy taxes on grain. The taxes on everyday items such as alcohol and salt were increased. The workers' wages were kept low. The government's idea was to squeeze the people hard and put all the money into industrial development. It was hoped that, once industry got going, everybody would become better off.

At first, things seemed to go well. Industry grew rapidly, especially iron and steel, and the railways. But then in 1902 there was an industrial slump and thousands of the new workers lost their jobs. Strikes and demonstrations broke out in many cities.

Disaster also struck in the countryside. There were poor harvests in 1900 and 1902. The peasants had already been squeezed to a point where they could barely survive. Now they were starving. There were outbreaks of violence and landlords' houses were burned.

The government's only solution to these problems was to use troops to crush any disturbances. But the demonstrations and violence continued throughout 1902 and 1903.

1. Why did Russia need to develop its industries?
2. a) How did the government plan to develop industries?
   b) Why did this plan run into difficulties?
   c) What were the effects of these difficulties?

The Russo-Japanese War

On top of all this, Russia got itself involved in a war with Japan in 1904. At first, Tsar Nicholas thought the war was a good idea. Victory in a short war would stop people criticising his government. But it was not long before the war made conditions worse than they had been before. Prices rose in the cities, as the war caused shortages of food and other goods. Lack of industrial materials caused factories to close, and more workers found themselves unemployed and hungry.

Even worse for the Tsar was that the Japanese inflicted defeat after defeat on the Russians. This was very humiliating, since Japan was such a small country in comparison with Russia. As the war progressed during 1904, Russia was pushed deeper and deeper into crisis. The year 1905 started very badly, when Port Arthur fell to the Japanese, bringing renewed protest about the incompetence of the Tsar and his government.

3. Why did a war break out with Japan (see Source 1)?
4. What attitude towards the war and the Japanese is shown in Source 2?
5. Why would this attitude make defeats in the war more shocking for the Russians?
6. What other effects did the war have?

The war started over a quarrel about land in Manchuria. Both Japan and Russia wanted control of this area. The Russians wanted Port Arthur because it was an ice-free port. Vladivostok, their main port on the Pacific Ocean, was cut off by ice for six months of the year.

RUSSIA
Trans-Siberian Railway
to Moscow
Chinese Eastern Railway
South Manchurian Railway
Vladivostok
Mukden
Tokyo
In March 1905 the Russia army was defeated at Mukden.
Peking
Port Arthur
KOREA
Tsushima Straits
JAPAN
CHINA
By January 1905 the Russians had surrendered at Port Arthur.
In May 1905 the Russian navy was destroyed in the Tsushima Straits. It had sailed half way round the world, taking six months to get to the war zone and was destroyed in under an hour.
0   500km

SOURCE 1 A map of the Russo-Japanese War, showing key events

18

SOURCE 2   A cartoon drawn during the Russo-Japanese War. The caption read 'Oh you funny Japs, always making mistakes. Thank you for the badly aimed shells which help me light my pipe!'

The spark: Bloody Sunday

At the beginning of 1905 conditions were bad in St Petersburg and tension was high. To ease the tension, a priest, Father Gapon, organised a march to deliver a petition to the Tsar, asking for his help.

SOURCE 3   Extracts from the workers' petition, organised by Father Gapon in 1905

❝ Sire – We, working men and inhabitants of St Petersburg, our wives and our children and our helpless old parents, come to You, Sire, to seek for truth, justice and protection. We have been made beggars, we are oppressed; we are near to death . . . The moment has come for us when death would be better than the prolongation of our intolerable sufferings . . . We ask but little: to reduce the working day to eight hours, to provide a minimum wage of a rouble a day . . .

Officials have brought the country to complete ruin and involved it in a shameful war. We working men have no voice in the way the enormous amounts raised from us in taxes are spent . . .

We are seeking here our last salvation. Do not refuse to help Your people. Destroy the wall between Yourself and Your people. ❞

On a cold, crisp morning, Sunday 22 January, some 200,000 people marched towards the Winter Palace to deliver the petition to the Tsar. As the marchers approached the palace, they were met by troops.

7. a) What were the workers asking the Tsar for in the petition (Source 3)?
    b) What does the petition tell you about the attitudes of the people towards the Tsar at this time?

SOURCE 4   From Leon Trotsky's book *1905*, written 1908–9. Trotsky was not in St Petersburg at the time

❝ As agreed, the march to the palace was a peaceful one, without songs, banners or speeches. People wore their Sunday clothes. In some parts of the city they carried icons and church banners. Everywhere the petitioners encountered troops. They begged to be allowed to pass. They wept, they tried to go around the barrier, they tried to break through it. ❞

What would happen next?

SOURCE 5 From *The Story of My Life*, 1905, by Father Gapon, the leader of the march

66 *Suddenly the company of Cossacks galloped rapidly towards us with drawn swords. So, then, it was to be a massacre after all! . . .*

A cry of alarm arose as the Cossacks came down upon us. Our front ranks broke before them, opening to the right and left, and down this lane the soldiers drove their horses, striking on both sides. I saw swords lifted and falling, the men, women and children dropping to the earth like logs of wood, while moans, curses and shouts filled the air . . .

Again we started forward, with solemn resolution and rising rage in our hearts. The Cossacks turned their horses and began to cut their way through the crowd from the rear. They passed through the whole column and galloped back towards the Narva Gate, where – the infantry having opened their ranks and let them through – they again formed line. We were still advancing . . .

We were not more than 30 yards from the soldiers, being separated from them only by the Tarakanovsky Canal, when suddenly, without warning and without a moment's delay, was heard the crack of many rifle shots. 99

1. Does Gapon's account of Bloody Sunday in Source 5 agree or disagree with the other sources? Give examples.
2. Look at how the people are represented in Source 7. What do you think were the aims of the artist who painted this picture?
3. Which are more useful to historians – the painting and photograph or the written sources? Explain your answer.
4. Source 6 is used in many history books to show troops firing on the crowds on Bloody Sunday. In fact it comes from a film about this event made in 1925. What questions do you need to ask about photographs in books?
5. Use Sources 3–8 to tell the story of Bloody Sunday.

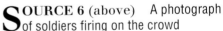

SOURCE 6 (above) A photograph of soldiers firing on the crowd

SOURCE 7 (left) A painting of soldiers firing on the crowd by Makovsky (1846–1920)

SOURCE 8 Trotsky (see Source 4)

66 *The soldiers fired all day long. The dead were counted in the hundreds, the wounded in the thousands. An exact count was impossible, since the police carted away and secretly buried the bodies at night.* 99

The consequences of Bloody Sunday

The estimated number of casualties on Bloody Sunday has varied from thousands to less than 100 (according to official government figures at the time). News of the massacre spread rapidly to other cities.

SOURCE 9 Written by the American consul in Odessa, 1905

66 *The present ruler has lost absolutely the affection of the Russian people, and whatever the future may have in store for the dynasty, the present Tsar will never again be safe in the midst of his people.* 99

SOURCE 10 By the French Consul in Kharkov, 1905

66 *Work stopped everywhere: on the railways, in all factories, workshops, in shops of all types, in the University, and all schools, in all administrative offices, even the telegraph offices . . . The whole population was on the streets, either as sightseers or as demonstrators . . . People began to ransack arms stores and to smash the windows of the large stores and conservative journals.*

Students, directed by lawyers, doctors and teachers, and helped by workmen and Jews . . . set up barricades. 99

6. How did Bloody Sunday change the way the people viewed the Tsar?

7. What were the other consequences of Bloody Sunday?

■ TASK

Bloody Sunday was the last straw. Within a week, a full-scale revolution was under way.

When we talk about the causes of an event, we often think about different types of causes:

- Long-term causes, which have been going on for a long time. *A*

- Short-term causes, which develop shortly before an event.

- Immediate causes, which act as a spark to start things happening. *C*

■ ACTIVITY

Write a short essay explaining the causes of the 1905 Revolution. Use the statements on the right as the basis for paragraphs in your essay and use the flow chart to give your essay a structure.

The statements below refer to causes of the 1905 Revolution. Put each one into one of the three categories of causes.

Bloody Sunday started the 1905 Revolution.

The peasants were very dissatisfied with their living conditions and how the land was divided up.

The workers had many grievances about their terrible working conditions. They wanted higher wages and shorter hours.

The people blamed the Tsar for losing the war with Japan. The war made already bad condtions in the cities even worse and brought the workers to breaking point.

The government's policies to develop industry had had disastrous effects on the people. This was made worse by poor harvests and an industrial slump.

Many middle-class people were angry that the Tsar would not share some of his power with the people.

The 1905 revolution

BY THE END of January, there were more than 400,000 workers out on strike. The 1905 Revolution was under way. For the rest of the year, the government had little control of events, as strikes, demonstrations, petitions, peasant uprisings, student riots and assassinations became commonplace. The Tsar was 'at war with his own people'.

1 In February, the strikes spread to other cities. Workers demanded an eight-hour day, higher wages and better conditions. On 4 February, the Tsar's uncle, the Grand Duke Sergei, was assassinated in Moscow.

2 In March and May, shameful defeats of the Russian army and navy in the war with Japan (see Source 1, page 18) led to demands for a change of government. In June sailors of the battleship *Potemkin* mutinied. This was very worrying for the government, as other sections of the armed forces might also mutiny.

3 By May and June, different groups were demanding changes. Middle-class liberals demanded an elected parliament, freedom of speech and the right to form political parties. National groups, like the Poles and Finns, demanded their independence. The Jews wanted equal civil rights.

4 In the countryside in June and July, peasant riots became widespread. Land was seized and landowners' houses were looted and burned.

5 In September, a peace treaty was signed between the Russians and the Japanese. Thousands of troops were now free to help put down the unrest in European Russia. The government paid them all their back pay and promised better conditions of service so that they would remain loyal to the Tsar.

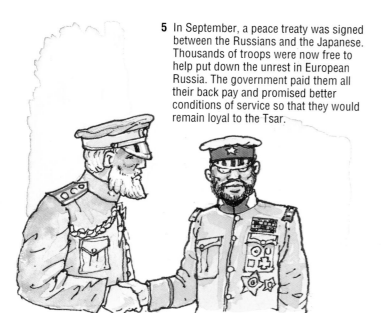

6 In October, a general strike spread from Moscow to other cities. All opposition groups – workers, students, teachers, doctors, revolutionaries – were united in demanding changes. Barricades were set up in the streets.

7 On 26 October, the St Petersburg Soviet of Workers' Deputies was formed. Representatives from factories met to co-ordinate strike action. Soviets were formed in other cities. This was a great threat to the Tsar's government.

8 The Tsar had the choice of giving in or using force, with the likelihood of massive bloodshed. He gave in and issued the **October Manifesto** on 30 October. **This promised**:
■ **a parliament or Duma elected by the people**
■ **civil rights – e.g. freedom of speech and conscience**
■ **uncensored newspapers and the right to form political parties.**
The liberals and middle classes believed they had won democratic government. They stopped their protests and supported the government.

9 By December, with all the troops back in Russia, the Tsar felt strong enough to take back control. He used force to close down the St Petersburg Soviet and crush an armed uprising in Moscow. He sent out troops to take revenge on workers and peasants who had rioted and bring them under control.

1. Draw a timeline for 1905, divided into months, to show the events of the year.
2. Take each of the following people in turn and write speech bubbles in which they say why they joined the protests and what they want:
■ an engineering worker
■ a peasant woman
■ a middle-class liberal lawyer
■ a Pole.
3. Choose three events or situations during 1905 which posed the greatest threat to the survival of the Tsar. Explain why you chose them. #7, #4, #3
4. What do you think were the main reasons why the Tsar survived the 1905 revolution? #8

23

Did life get better for Russian people after 1905?

THE TSAR SURVIVED the 1905 Revolution with the opportunity to make changes and to carry out the promises he had made. He managed to stay in power for another twelve years, but in 1917 he was forced to abdicate. Some historians think the First World War was the reason for this and that without the war he would have survived. Others argue that he was heading for disaster anyway. See what you think.

1. Who do you think is riding the horse in Source 1?
2. What is the attitude of the cartoonist to what was going on in Russia?

Order and control

Although most of the trouble in the cities had stopped by the end of 1905, violent disturbances continued in the countryside well into 1906. The Tsar appointed Peter Stolypin as Prime Minister to deal with this. He had a reputation for being tough. He set up military courts, which could sentence and hang a person on the spot. Thousands were executed by these courts, and the hangman's noose became known as 'Stolypin's necktie'.

The Okhrana, the secret police, were still very active, with thousands of informers. Everybody had to carry internal passports and travellers had to register with the police outside their home districts. Freedom of the press had been guaranteed in 1905, but newspapers were often fined for writing articles offending the government, and frequently newspapers appeared with white spaces where material had been censored.

SOURCE 1 A cartoon captioned *Peace and Quiet*, 1906

The Dumas

At the end of 1905, the Tsar had given way to demands for a parliament or DUMA elected by the people. But would it have any power, and how would it be elected? By the time the first Duma met in April 1906, the answers to these questions were clear. The Duma could not pass laws, could not appoint ministers and could not control finance in important areas such as defence, and the Tsar could dissolve it whenever he wished. Elections favoured the nobles: there was one representative for every 2,000 nobles, but one for every 90,000 workers.

Despite this, the first two Dumas of 1906 and 1907 were very radical, demanding more power for themselves and rights for ordinary people (e.g. freedom to strike, free education). They also demanded that more land should be given to the

SOURCE 2   What Nicholas said about the Duma in 1908

❝ *I created the Duma not to have it instruct me, but to have it advise me.* ❞

SOURCE 3   Count Kokovstov gives an eye-witness account of the opening of the Duma in the Tauride Palace on 26 April 1906

❝ *The entire right side of the room was filled with uniformed people . . . the Tsar's retinue. The left side was crowded with the members of the Duma . . . the overwhelming majority . . . dressed in workers' blouses and cotton shirts, and behind them was a crowd of peasants in the most varied costumes, some in national dress.*

. . . The first place among these representatives of the people was occupied by a man tall in stature, dressed in a worker's blouse and high, oiled boots, who examined the throne and those about it with a derisive and insolent air . . . P.A. Stolypin turned to me and said, 'I even have a feeling that this man might throw a bomb.' ❞

peasants. The Tsar would have none of this and dissolved both Dumas after a few weeks.

For the third Duma, Stolypin changed the way the members were elected to favour the gentry and urban rich even more. As a result, the third Duma was much more conservative. Even so, this Duma, which lasted from 1907 to 1912, was often critical of the government, and some good measures were passed on matters to do with the army and navy and accident insurance for workers. The fourth Duma (1912–14) achieved little before war was declared, but at least the Tsar was starting to work with it.

3. What power did the Duma have?
4. From the information in Sources 2 and 3:
a) Do you think the Duma had much chance of working successfully with the Tsar?
b) Whose fault do you think this was?

Changes in the countryside

To try to make agriculture more efficient, Stolypin introduced reforms to encourage the 'best elements' amongst the peasantry.

Peasants were allowed to buy up strips of land from their less enterprising neighbours to make one single land holding, which they owned individually. Stolypin

Diagram 1   A village before Stolypin's land reforms

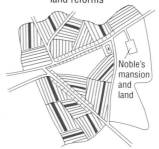

Peasants held land in strips.

━━ = strips held by one household

☐ = houses

Diagram 2   The same village after the reforms

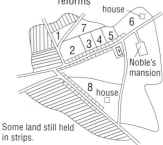

Some land still held in strips.

1–5 and 7 show blocks of land where one peasant's strips have been put together as a block.

Some peasants bought strips from poorer neighbours to form larger blocks (6 and 8). These peasants were called 'kulaks'.

SOURCE 4   Stolypin's land reform

set up a peasants' bank to provide loans for them to do this. He believed that peasants would want to improve their own land and use modern methods to produce more food. He also hoped this would create a new class of prosperous landowning peasants – KULAKS – who would be loyal to the government.

About fifteen per cent of peasants took up his offer and there were improvements. Production of grain did increase and there was a record harvest in 1913. Unfortunately, the outbreak of war in 1914 interrupted the reforms. The reforms did, however, have another consequence: a lot of poorer peasants were forced to sell their land and became labourers, wandering around the countryside seeking work. Some went to work in the cities, but many remained in the countryside, with not even a small patch of land to support their families.

Around four million peasants were encouraged by the government to settle on new lands along the Trans-Siberian Railway. They made long journeys, crammed into wagons, but when they arrived they found that the best land had been taken by rich land speculators. Over half of them returned to European Russia, very angry that they had been misled and with nothing to go back to.

5. Stolypin called his policy a 'wager on the strong and sober' among the peasants. What do you think he meant by this and why did he think this would solve problems in agriculture?
6. What consequences of the reforms could prove dangerous for the government?
7. Which peasants would think their situation was improving in 1914 and which would think it was getting worse?

Changes in the cities

Between 1906 and 1914, there was an industrial boom in Russia. Between 1905 and 1914, total industrial production increased by 100 per cent. Russia became the world's fourth largest producer of coal, pig iron and steel. The Baku oil fields were rivalled only by those in Texas. Many of the factories were very efficient, using the most up-to-date mass-production methods.

By 1914, two-fifths of factory workers were in factories with over 1,000 workers. This made the factories more efficient, but it also made it easier to organise strikes.

However, the workers did not benefit much from the boom. Working conditions improved little, if at all, over the period. Average wages were, in real terms, below the pitiful levels of 1903. Prices had risen so much that workers could only just manage to buy the bread they needed.

In 1912, an important strike took place in the Lena goldfields in Siberia. Striking workers protested about degrading working conditions, low wages and a working day which lasted from 5.00 a.m. to 7.00 p.m. They clashed with troops, and 170 workers were killed and 373 wounded. The Lena Goldfield Massacre had a similar effect to Bloody Sunday in 1905 and opened the floodgates for workers' protests.

1. a) What does Source 5 tell you about changes in Russian cities?
b) What pressures might this create?
2. Study Source 6.
a) What is the pattern of strikes between 1905 and 1914?
b) What does the pattern for political strikes tell you?
3. What reasons can you suggest for the strikes?
4. Who, according to Source 7, was benefiting from the industrial boom?

■ ACTIVITY

Work in pairs. One of you must argue that things were improving in Russia before 1914, using the evidence from pages 24–26 to support this view. The other side must collect evidence to put the opposite case. Try to come to some agreement at the end of your discussion, then write your own balanced account of whether life was improving before 1914 or not.

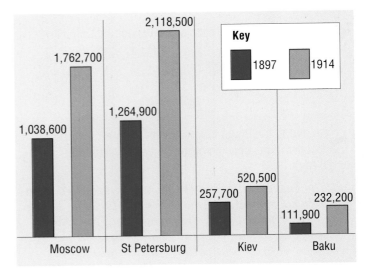

SOURCE 5 Populations of major cities in 1897 and 1914

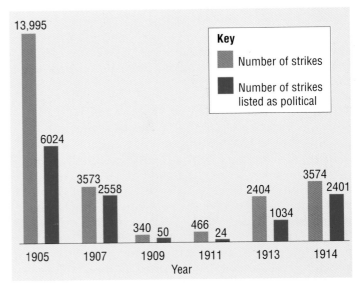

SOURCE 6 Ministry of Trade and Industry figures on strikes in workplaces covered by factory inspection

SOURCE 7 Alexei Tolstoy describes St Petersburg before 1914

66 *In the last ten years huge enterprises had sprung into being with unbelievable rapidity. Fortunes of millions of roubles appeared as if out of thin air . . . People doped themselves with music . . . with half-naked women . . . with champagne. Gambling clubs, theatres, picture houses, amusement parks cropped up like mushrooms . . . Everything was accessible: the women no less than the riches.* 99

Rasputin: sex maniac or holy man?

ONE OF THE most fascinating episodes in the period before the war was the arrival of Grigory Rasputin at the royal court. Rasputin was a starets (a holy man) from Siberia. It was rumoured he belonged to a religious sect, the Kylysty, who believed that the way to religious ecstasy lay in the senses. Men and women flogged themselves and sometimes engaged in sexual acts.

Rasputin organised gatherings which attracted women from the higher circles of society. Many came to him seeking advice or healing – and later favours, when he became a friend of the royal family. There were stories of wild drunken parties and orgies, and of Rasputin seducing women with his hypnotic powers.

To what extent these stories were true is not clear. Rasputin had many enemies. Was he the coarse, uncouth, smelly peasant that some made him out to be? It does seem that his weakness was sex and that he had a string of lovers. But did they include the Tsarina and her two eldest daughters as rumour had it?

It is his relationship with the Tsar and Tsarina that makes his story important. The Tsar's son, Alexis, was a haemophiliac. This meant that his blood did not clot easily. Cuts and even bruises could lead to long bouts of bleeding, which caused him severe pain. In 1907, it was thought that he was dying, and Rasputin was called in. After Rasputin's visit, Alexis started to recover. The Tsarina, a very religious woman, was convinced that Rasputin had been sent by God to save her son. Rasputin became a close friend of the royal family.

How Rasputin helped Alexis is not known. It may be that he had skill with herbs and medicines, or some mastery of hypnosis. Whatever he did, it was effective, or thought to be so. In 1912, a famous incident took place when Alexis was seriously ill and Rasputin was not in St Petersburg. On hearing of Alexis' plight, Rasputin sent a telegram saying that Alexis would recover on the following day – and, apparently, he did.

The Tsar and Tsarina's reputation suffered from their association with Rasputin, the most talked-of man in St Petersburg. The relationship shocked the highest levels of government and society. It also soured relations with Stolypin, the Tsar's most able minister. Stolypin had Rasputin banished from St Petersburg, much to the Tsarina's fury. But after Stolypin's death in 1912, Rasputin returned and his influence increased.

This brought the Tsar into conflict with the Duma and the press. Articles about Rasputin were censored, which was not only seen as an attack on the freedom of the press, but of course also increased the gossip. The Rasputin connection had serious repercussions for the Tsar, and matters were to get worse during the First World War.

■ SOURCE INVESTIGATION

What was the truth about Rasputin?

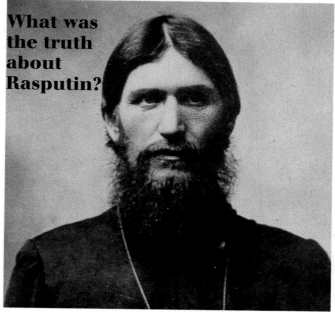

SOURCE 1   A photograph of Rasputin

SOURCE 2   From the memoirs of the French Ambassador at the time, Maurice Paleologue

66 *Brown hair, long and ill-combed; a black stiff beard; a high forehead; a large, jutting nose; a powerful mouth. But the whole expression of the face was concentrated in the eyes – flax-blue eyes, of a strange brilliance, depth and fascination. Their glance was at the same time piercing and caressing, ingenuous and astute, direct and remote. When his speech became animated, his pupils seemed to be charged with magnetism.* 99

SOURCE 3   A description of Rasputin by Stolypin, the Tsar's chief minister, who disapproved of him

66 *He ran his pale eyes over me, mumbled mysterious and inarticulate words from the Scriptures, made strange movements with his hands, and I began to feel an indescribable loathing for the vermin sitting opposite me. Still, I did realise that the man possessed great hypnotic power.* 99

1. Use Sources 1–3 to explain the impression Rasputin created.

SOURCE 4 A photograph of Rasputin surrounded by 'ladies of the aristocracy'. It was published in newspapers in Europe and America, suggesting that this was Rasputin's aristocratic harem

SOURCE 7 Part of a letter to the newspaper *Golos Moskvy* from the editor of a religious paper

". . . the cry of indignation that bursts forth from the lips of all Orthodox men and women against that cunning conspirator against our Holy Church, that fornicator of souls and bodies – Grigory Rasputin . . . in all the letters they send me, they describe this propagator of false doctrine as a sex maniac and a charlatan."

SOURCE 5 Michael Rodzianko, a president of the Duma, became a fierce enemy of Rasputin. He said he had received many letters from the mothers of women who had been dishonoured by Rasputin. He quoted this story, told by a woman who went to ask Rasputin to help her husband

"He [Rasputin] scolded me severely and said, 'Aren't you ashamed? Come to me to repent, but with your shoulders bare' . . . He pierced me with his gaze and took liberties with me, so I left, indignant, deciding not to approach him again. However, anxious and worried, disturbed, too – fascinated, in short – I obtained a low-cut dress and, pale-faced, went to see him . . . A few days later my husband got his promotion."

SOURCE 6 Secret police reports for 1912 have entries such as the following

"■ On the night of 17 January, Maria Gill, wife of a captain in the 145th Regiment, slept at Rasputin's.
■ On the night of 25 November, Varvarova, the actress, slept at Rasputin's.
■ Rasputin came home in the motor car . . . with the prostitute Gregubova . . . He was blind drunk, kissed Gregubova passionately and stroked her cheeks."

SOURCE 8 Letters from the Tsarina to Rasputin were stolen and found their way to the press and public. Some historians think her letters were altered. This is from one of them

"My beloved, unforgettable teacher, redeemer, mentor! How tiresome it is without you. My soul is quiet and I relax only when you, my teacher, are sitting beside me. I kiss your hands and lean my blessed shoulders . . . I wish only one thing: to fall asleep . . . for ever on your shoulders and in your arms . . . Will you soon be again close to me? Come quickly, I am waiting for you and I am tormenting myself for you . . . I love you for ever."

SOURCE 9 By Anna Vyroubova, a loyal friend of the Tsarina and, some claimed, Rasputin's lover

"Rasputin had no harem at Court. In fact I cannot remotely imagine a woman of education and refinement being attracted to him in a personal way. I never knew of one being attracted, and although accusations of secret debauchery with women of the lower classes were made against him . . . the police were never able to bring forward one woman of any class whom they could accuse with Rasputin. The photograph [Source 4] is authentic, I figure in it and can explain it. It shows a group of women and men who, after attending early Mass, sometimes gathered round Rasputin for religious discourse, for advice on all manner of things . . . Many lovelorn women (and men) used to go to those meetings to beg his prayers on their heart's behalf."

SOURCE 10 From the report of a commission led by Vladimir Roudenev, which investigated aspects of the Tsarist regime, including Rasputin, after the Revolution in March 1917

"From the reports of the secret police, it was found that his love affairs consisted solely of night orgies with music-hall singers and an occasional petitioner. Of his relations with women of high society nothing was established, either by the police records or by information acquired by the commission.

Rasputin was a man of large heart. He kept open house, and his lodgings were always crowded with a curiously mixed company . . . The investigation disclosed an immense amount of evidence concerning the petitions carried by Rasputin to Court, but all of these . . . referred merely to applications for positions, favours, railway concessions and the like. "

1. What does Source 8 suggest about the relationship between Rasputin and the Tsarina?
2. Do you think that some of these sources are more reliable than others?
   a) Choose two sources which you do not trust and explain why.
   b) Choose two sources which you do trust and explain why.
3. Either
   a) Use the evidence in Sources 4–8 to put the case against Rasputin, showing what a scandalous person he was.
      Or
   b) Use Sources 9 and 10 to defend him. You could also give reasons for not trusting Sources 4–8.
4. What are your conclusions about Rasputin? Do you think he was as bad as he is made out to be?
5. Discuss the following statement: 'It does not matter what the truth about Rasputin was. People like to believe scandal and rumours, especially about royalty. It was the effect all this had on the reputation of the Tsar and Tsarina that mattered.'

The death of Rasputin

In December 1916, Prince Yusupov, who was related to the Tsar, decided to get rid of Rasputin because of the damage he was doing to the reputation of the royal family. He invited Rasputin to a party at his home, with several friends who were also in on the plot. Taking him to a room downstairs, Yusupov fed him wine and cakes laced with arsenic. He waited for Rasputin to die, but nothing happened. In frustration, Yusupov shot Rasputin in the back with a revolver. But about half an hour later, according to Yusupov:

. . . his right eyelid began to quiver, then opened. I then saw both eyes – the green eyes of a viper – staring at me with an expression of diabolical hatred. The blood ran cold in my veins. My muscles turned to stone.

Then a terrible thing happened: with a sudden violent effort Rasputin leapt to his feet, foaming at the mouth. A wild roar echoed through the vaulted rooms, and his hands convulsively thrashed at the air. He rushed at me, trying to get at my throat, and sank his fingers into my shoulder like steel claws. His eyes were bursting from their sockets, blood oozed from his lips. And all the time he called me by name, in a low, raucous voice.

Yusupov ran up the stairs, followed by Rasputin scrambling on his hands and knees. As Rasputin stumbled out of the house, one of Yusupov's friends shot him several times. Yusupov then rushed up with a club and battered Rasputin until he was sure he was dead. They then tied up the body and took it to the frozen River Neva nearby. They cut a hole in the ice and pushed him through. When the body was recovered three days later, it was reported that Rasputin had untied himself and that there was ice under his fingernails where he had tried to claw his way out from underneath the ice.

1. Yusupov wrote his story some years after the event. How do you think this may have affected it?
2. Why do you think he was so determined to kill Rasputin?

■ ACTIVITY

Write a story about Rasputin in the style of a tabloid newspaper of today. Explain who Rasputin is, what he has been getting up to, and how this is affecting the reputation of the royal family. You can hint at his relationship with the Tsarina.

WHEN WAR BROKE out against Germany in 1914, the Tsar became more popular than he had been for years. The Russian people united in their support for him: problems could be set aside in the face of a common enemy. Crowds cheered the Tsar as troops paraded past him on the way to the war front. St Petersburg was renamed the more Russian-sounding Petrograd (*grad* means town in Russian, whereas *burg* means town in German).

Another positive result of the outbreak of war was that the Tsar started to work more closely with the Duma. Able people from the Duma began to be appointed to important posts.

1. Why was the outbreak of war a good thing for the Tsar?
2. What impressions do Sources 1 and 2 give you of the support for the Tsar?
3. What expectations do you think the Russian people had of him at the beginning of the war?

SOURCE 1 Written by Muriel Buchanan (daughter of the British Ambassador to Russia) on the outbreak of war

66 *The processions in the street carrying the Tsar's portrait, framed in the flags of the allies, the bands everywhere playing the national anthem . . . the long unending line of khaki-clad figures who marched away singing and cheering, tall bronzed men with honest, open faces with childlike eyes and a trusting faith in the little father [the Tsar], and a sure and certain hope that the saints would protect them and bring them back to their villages.*

. . . Those first days of war! How full we were of enthusiasm, of the conviction that we were fighting in a just and holy cause . . . 99

SOURCE 2 Written by the *Times* correspondent in July 1914, on witnessing a huge crowd in front of the Winter Palace

66 *At last the Tsar, moved by the magnitude of the demonstration, appears on the balcony over-looking the square. Instantly the throng sinks upon its knees and with absolute spontaneity sings the deep-throated Russian anthem. For perhaps the first time since Napoleon's invasion of Russia the people and their Tsar were one, and the strength that unity spreads in a nation stirred throughout the Empire.* 99

SOURCE 3 A map of the Eastern Front, showing the first battles. Russia and its allies, Britain and France, were fighting against Germany and the Austro-Hungarian Empire

Step 1: The effects of the war on the soldiers

Enthusiasm for the war did not last for long. After some initial successes against the Austrians, the Russians were heavily defeated by the Germans at Tannenberg and the Masurian Lakes. Losses mounted rapidly – over one million soldiers were killed, wounded or taken prisoner by the end of 1914, and this number had risen to eight million by March 1917.

Soldiers saw their comrades being slaughtered in a futile manner. Many died without weapons or ammunition, and some did not even have boots to wear in the bitterly cold weather. They blamed their officers, who appeared unfeeling and ineffective. And things got worse as the war went on.

■ SOURCE INVESTIGATION

What was the state of the Russian army?

SOURCE 4   From a report by Michael Rodzianko, President of the Duma, on a visit to the war front

❝ The army had neither wagons nor horses nor first aid supplies . . . We visited the Warsaw station, where there were about 17,000 men wounded in battles. At the station we found a terrible scene: on the platform in dirt, filth and cold, in the rain, on the ground, even without straw, wounded, who filled the air with heart-rending cries, dolefully asked: 'For God's sake order them to dress our wounds, for five days we have not been attended to.' ❞

Rodzianko's son fought in the army

❝ Our son . . . began to narrate his experiences. Criminal incompetence, lack of co-operation in the higher command . . . had resulted in slackness of our crack regiments.

Rodzianko told the story of a frontal attack on the Rai-Mestro heights, ordered by a Grand Duke who had been told not to attack from the front because of a swamp

The troops found themselves in a swamp, where many men perished . . . My son sank up to his armpits, and was with difficulty extricated . . . The wounded could not be brought out, and perished in the swamp. Our artillery fire was weak . . . the shells fell short and dropped among our own men . . . Nevertheless, the gallant guards fulfilled their task, though bled white, and succeeded in capturing the heights, WHICH THEY WERE THEN ORDERED TO ABANDON. ❞

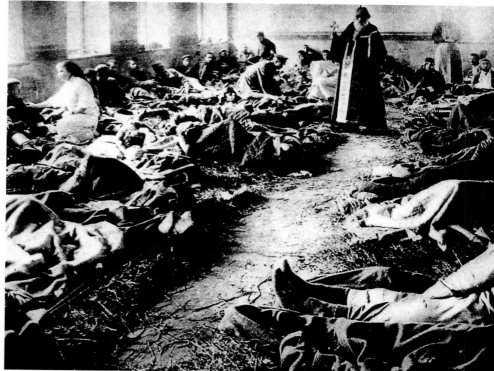

SOURCE 5   A priest blessing the wounded

SOURCE 6   Written by General Belaiev

❝ In recent battles, a third of the men had no rifles. The poor devils had to wait patiently until their comrades fell before their eyes and they could pick up weapons. The army is drowning in its own blood. ❞

SOURCE 7   By the Chairman of the Military Commission of the Duma

❝ As early as the beginning of the second year of the war desertions [of soldiers] at the front and on their way to the front became commonplace, and the average number of deserters reached 25 per cent. I happen to know of three cases when the train was stopped because there were no passengers on it; all, with the exception of the officer in command, had run away. ❞

4. Why was the morale of the soldiers so low?
5. What do Sources 4–7 tell us about the problems of the army?
6. Which do you think was the most worrying problem? Why?

Step 2: The effects of the war on the Russians at home

1 Food was getting short. Millions of male peasants had been conscripted into the army, so there was a shortage of farm workers and less food was being produced. In addition, food was not getting to the cities: the Russian railway system was being used to carry supplies to the war front, and so trains carrying food to the cities had been reduced.

2 Coal and industrial materials were short. Many factories closed, making their workers unemployed. The lack of coal and fuel in general meant that people in the cities were cold as well as hungry.

3 Because of the shortages, the prices of goods were rising continually, but wages were hardly going up at all. To make matters worse, workers were being asked to work longer hours. And to add insult to injury, the sale of vodka was stopped during the war.

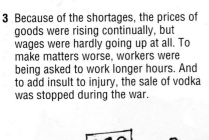

4 Factories closed, leading to unemployment and even greater poverty.

As defeat piled on defeat and the number of casualties increased, Russians in the cities began to lose confidence in the government. They were also suffering from the economic effects of the war.

1. Make a list of the reasons why people in the cities were getting more and more unhappy about the war.

We fought side by side, but a shell landed next to him.

Step 3: Turning point – a terrible mistake

I'm going to the war front. You run things here while I'm away.

SOURCE 8 A cartoon of Rasputin with the Tsar and Tsarina

In the midst of these difficulties, Nicholas II made a terrible mistake: in September 1915, he decided to take over the running of the war and to go to the war front himself. This had serious consequences. Firstly, Nicholas himself was now blamed for defeats in the war. Secondly, the Tsar handed over the day-to-day running of the country to the Tsarina. The people mistrusted her because of her German background, and thought she was a spy. Her close relationship with Rasputin contributed further to the collapse of her reputation. He seemed to be in charge of the government. There were stories that they were lovers.

The Tsarina made a mess of running the country. She would not work with the Duma at all. She dismissed able ministers and replaced them with 'our men', meaning men who would do what they were told or who were friends of Rasputin. Some were incompetent and others downright scoundrels. There were so many changes of ministers that nobody was organising food, fuel and other supplies for the cities properly. The railway system fell into chaos and trainloads of food were left rotting in the sidings.

2. What is the message of the cartoon in Source 8?
3. How do Sources 8 and 9 show the damage being done by the Tsarina and Rasputin?

SOURCE 9 Part of a letter from the Tsarina to Nicholas at the war front

66 *Deary, I heard that that horrid Rodzianko wants the Duma to be called together – oh please don't, it's not their business, they want to discuss things not concerning them and bring more discontent – they must be kept away . . .*

Listen to our friend [Rasputin] . . . it is not for nothing God sent him to us . . . we must pay attention to what he says . . . Forgive me, but I don't like the choice of the Minister of War, Polianov . . . is he not our friend's [Rasputin's] enemy? 99

Step 4: Losing support

SOURCE 12   A bread queue in Moscow, September 1917

As the news from the war got worse and the situation in the cities got more desperate, support for the Tsar and his wife began to decrease among the middle and upper classes of society, and even among the aristocracy. They were appalled that a man like Rasputin should be allowed such influence, and they had little respect for the Tsarina. They blamed the Tsar for allowing this situation to develop.

The winter of 1916 was a bad one. The railway lines were so iced up that hardly any food or fuel got into Petrograd. Prices went sky high. Huge bread queues formed, but often there was no bread.

SOURCE 10   Written by Sir Henry Wilson in Petrograd, February 1917

❝ . . . as certain as anything that the Emperor and Empress are riding for a fall. Everyone – officers, merchants, ladies – talks openly of the absolute necessity of doing away with them. ❞

SOURCE 11   A police report made at the end of 1916

❝ The industrial PROLETARIAT of the capital is on the verge of despair . . . the smallest outbreak will lead to uncontrollable riots . . . Even if we assume that wages have increased by 100 per cent, the cost of living has risen by 300 per cent. The impossibility of obtaining food, the time wasted in spending hours waiting in queues outside shops, the increasing death rate due to inadequate diet and anti-sanitary lodgings, cold and dampness as a result of lack of coal and firewood – all these conditions have created such a situation that the mass of industrial workers are quite ready to let themselves go to the wildest excesses of a hunger riot . . . ❞

SOURCE 13   A demonstration on International Women's Day, 8 March

1. Why would the statement in Source 10 be very worrying for the Tsar?
2. What do Sources 11 and 12 show us about the state of Russian cities at the end of 1916? Why were people getting angry?

Step 5: The revolution begins

By March 1917 the situation had become desperate and there was a serious mood of discontent. The workers wanted political changes as well as food and fuel.

On 7 March in Petrograd, 40,000 workers from the giant Putilov engineering works went on strike for higher wages. The next day was International Women's Day and thousands of women joined strikers in demonstrations all over the city, shouting 'Down with hunger! Bread for the workers!' (see Source 13). In the two days that followed, thousands of workers, men and women, joined in demanding food, fuel and better conditions, and a new government.

The Tsar ordered that the demonstrations be put down by force. After all, there had been riots before. Rodzianko, leader of the Duma, sent a telegram saying that the situation was at crisis point. The Tsar commented to a minister, 'That fat Rodzianko has again sent me some nonsense to which I will not even bother to reply.' The Tsar was wrong not to take any notice.

Step 6: The army takes sides

12 March was a decisive day and changed the character of the riots. Soldiers in Petrograd refused to fire on crowds, and some regiments shot their officers and joined in the demonstrations. They had had enough of the war and the way they were treated. This made the demonstrations of 1917 different from anything that had gone before.

The soldiers joined the strikers and the women in the streets and marched to the Duma to demand that it take control of the government.

> **S**OURCE 14   Report by an agent of the Okhrana (secret police), 11 March 1917
>
> **66***Everything depends on the behaviour of the military units; if the latter do not join the proletariat, the movement will quickly subside: but if the troops turn against the government, then nothing can save the country from a revolutionary upheaval.* **99**

> **S**OURCE 15   A diary entry for 12 March 1917 by Shulgin, a Duma deputy
>
> **66***During the last few days we have been living, as it were, on a volcano . . . It is not, of course, a question of bread. The trouble is that in that large city it is impossible to find a few hundred people who feel kindly towards the government.* **99**

3. On what, according to Sources 14 and 15, did the revolution depend?

Step 7: The Tsar abdicates

Nicholas tried to get back to Petrograd, but it was too late. Railway workers refused to let his train into the city. It was from his train that, on 15 March, the Tsar finally decided to abdicate in favour of his brother Michael. (Alexis, his son, was too ill to be Tsar.) But the people had had enough of the royal family.

1. What does Source 16 tell us about the people's attitude to the Tsar at the end of his reign?

SOURCE 16   A photograph showing the head of a statue of the Tsar on the ground

■ ACTIVITY

You are going to write an essay with the title 'What were the causes of the Russian Revolution in March 1917?'.
Use the chart below to plan your essay. Make a copy on a large piece of paper. Make brief notes in each section about what you want to include.

CAUSES OF THE REVOLUTION OF MARCH 1917			
Before the war			
Economic causes How well were industry and agriculture doing?	*Social causes* Had the conditions of a) the workers and b) the peasants improved in the years leading up to the war?		*Political causes* Were people's views being heard through the Duma? How well was the Tsar running the country?
The war			
Effects of the war . . . on people	*Effects of the war . . . on the army*	*The Tsar's mistakes*	*The role of the Tsarina and Rasputin*
The Revolution			
Conditions in March 1917		*Crucial role of the army*	
Conclusions: Weigh up the importance of different causes			
Was the war the main cause?		*Were the failures of the Tsar before and during the war the main cause?*	

HOW DID THE BOLSHEVIKS TAKE OVER AND HOW DID THEY HOLD ON TO POWER?

chapter 4

WHY WERE THE BOLSHEVIKS ABLE TO SEIZE POWER IN NOVEMBER 1917?

Did the Provisional Government rule Russia well?

March

12 Formation of Provisional Government and Petrograd Soviet

14 Order No. 1 issued by the Soviet

16 Tsar abdicates. Provisional Government declared

April

16 Lenin returns to Petrograd from Switzerland

17 April Theses published

May

5 Non-Bolshevik Socialists become ministers in the Provisional Government

June

15 First all-Russian Congress of Soviets meets

July

2 Major military offensive launched by Kerensky

16–19 July Days. Lenin goes into hiding in Finland

September

15 Attempted coup by General Kornilov

19 Bolsheviks win control of Moscow Soviet

October

6 Bolsheviks win control of Petrograd Soviet

23 Lenin returns to Petrograd secretly and persuades Bolsheviks to seize power

November

6–7 Bolsheviks take control of Petrograd and force out the Provisional Government

A question of dates

In 1917 Russia still used the Julian calendar. This was 13 days behind the Gregorian calendar used in the rest of Europe. This is important because it can cause confusion when talking about the two revolutions in 1917.

1. The February/March revolution took place between 23 and 27 February according to the old Russian dates, but 8 to 12 March on the modern calendar.
2. The October/November revolution took place on 26 October according to the old dates, but 7 November on the modern calendar.

The Communists changed to the modern calendar in 1918. In this book the modern calendar dates are used – we talk of the March and November revolutions. But many books (and Russians) talk of the February and October revolutions.

SOURCE 1 A timeline of events from March to November 1917

The Tauride Palace

The Provisional Government

Who was going to rule Russia now that the Tsar had been thrown out? Crowds gathered outside the Tauride Palace, demanding that the Duma take charge. Inside, the members of the Duma were worried and frightened. What if generals loyal to the Tsar arrived with troops to execute them for treason? Some slipped away into the crowds and left the city. Those remaining discussed and argued long into the night.

They decided to form a temporary government – a Provisional Government. This would run the country until elections could be held to choose a government and decide how Russia was to be ruled in the future.

The Soviet

As the Provisional Government was being formed, another body, the Petrograd Soviet, was taking shape in a different part of the same building. Workers and soldiers sent representatives to form a soviet to look after their interests. In the next few weeks, soviets appeared all over Russia, but the Petrograd Soviet was the most important. The first thing the Soviet did was to issue Order No. 1, which gave it control of the armed forces in Petrograd.

SOURCE 2   A postcard, published in 1917, showing the main members of the Provisional Government. Prince Lvov, a liberal, became the leader. The rest of the government was mainly made up of middle-class liberals

SOURCE 3   A photograph of the members of the Petrograd Soviet

Dual Power

It was a strange situation: the Provisional Government was accepted as the government, but it could carry out its decisions only if the Soviet agreed. Most people were in favour of the first measures taken by the new government. Political prisoners were freed, and the government announced that there would be freedom of the press, freedom of speech, the right to strike and an end to social discrimination and the death penalty. Russians had more freedom now than they had had for centuries.

SOURCE 4 A letter from Guchkov, Minister for War in the Provisional Government, to General Alekseev, 22 March 1917

❝ The Provisional Government possesses no real power and its orders are executed only in so far as this is permitted by the Soviet of Workers' and Soldiers' Deputies, which holds in its hands the most important elements of actual power, such as troops, railroads, postal and telegraph service . . . ❞

SOURCE 5 Extracts from Order No.1, adapted from *Source Book of Russian History*, vol. 3, by Vernadsky

❝ The Soviet of Workers' and Soldiers' Deputies has decided:

- *In all companies, battalions, squadrons and separate branches of military service of all kinds and on warships, committees . . . should be chosen immediately.*
- *The orders of . . . the State Duma [Provisional Government] shall be carried out only . . . [when] they do not contradict the orders and decisions of the Soviet of Workers' and Soldiers' Deputies.*
- *All kinds of arms, such as rifles and machine guns, must be . . . under the control of the company and battalion committees and must in no case be handed over to officers even at their demand.*
- *. . . the addressing of officers with titles such as 'Your Excellency', 'Your Honour', etc. is abolished and these titles are replaced by . . . 'Mr General', 'Mr Colonel' and so on . . . ❞*

Alexander Kerensky

SOURCE 6 A photograph of Alexander Kerensky

A key person in these events was Alexander Kerensky. He had become involved in revolutionary activities as a young man but he had turned to the Socialist Revolutionaries rather than the Marxists. He had been elected to the Duma in 1912 and was famous for his emotional speeches, which the public loved.

It was Kerensky who met the crowds outside the Duma to discuss their demands and then helped persuade the Duma members to form the Provisional Government, in which he was made Minister of Justice. But he also became a member of the Petrograd Soviet. He went to meetings of both bodies, making sure that they understood each other. He was the bridge between them.

As 1917 progressed, Kerensky became more and more important, becoming first Minister for War and, at the end of July, Prime Minister. His powers of speech-making were put to great effect: in mass meetings for the war effort, women threw jewels at his feet. His actions were to be very important in deciding how matters turned out in Russia.

1. How do Sources 2–5 show:
   a) the differences between the Provisional Government and the Soviet?
   b) who held the power?
   c) what the Soviet controlled?
2. What sections of Order No. 1 would be particularly worrying for the Provisional Government?
3. Why is it difficult for a government to rule effectively if it cannot get its decisions carried out?
4. Why was Kerensky (see panel) so important in the early days of the Revolution?

Two big issues faced the Provisional Government after the Revolution, and its survival depended on how it handled these.

Issue 1: War

The Provisional Government, with the agreement of the Soviet, decided to continue the war. Nobody wanted to be defeated by the Germans and they knew that the Germans would make them pay a heavy price if they tried to make peace. Also the Provisional Government wanted to keep the Allies – France and Britain – on their side for help in the future.

But the war continued to go badly, and soldiers began to desert in ever-increasing numbers. Food and fuel remained short as the war drained the country's resources. The people desperately wanted it to end.

SOURCE 7   A photograph showing soldiers deserting the front

SOURCE 9   A housekeeper speaking on 17 April, quoted in *The Russian Revolution of 1917, A Personal Record* by N. Sukanov

" The queues, well the queues haven't got any smaller in the least; I think they're even bigger. You stand half the day just as before . . . it's all the same, there's nothing to be had. They say it's just the same, 'The rich keep on fleecing the poor. The shopkeepers are the only ones making money.' "

Issue 2: Land

With the Tsar gone, the peasants believed that at last they could achieve their dream – to own their land. But the Provisional Government would not give it to them. It felt that this was such an important issue that it should be left to the properly elected government of Russia. They were also worried that a free-for-all for land would lead to the disintegration of the army, because the soldiers, most of whom were peasants, would desert to get their share. However, as 1917 went on, the peasants began taking the land for themselves whatever the government said.

SOURCE 8   The Women's Death Battalion was formed (to shame deserters) in July 1917 by Maria Bocharyova, a remarkable woman soldier who had been wounded three times. The top photo shows the battalion being blessed by a priest

5. Were the conditions in the cities much better after the Revolution?
6. Why did the peasants not support the Provisional Government?
7. Why did the people so desperately want the war to end?

How did the Bolsheviks seize power?

Lenin returns

THE ARRIVAL OF Lenin, leader of the Bolsheviks, was to change the whole course of the revolution. Lenin had been in Switzerland when the March Revolution took place, and at first he could not get back to Russia as he had to cross Germany, where the Russians were fighting. However, the Germans were pleased to help him, hoping that he would cause trouble for the Russian government. They gave him money and put him in a special sealed train, which travelled through Germany to Finland. He then made his way to Petrograd, arriving at the beginning of April.

The Germans were right. Lenin did cause a stir and he did make trouble. Immediately on his arrival he made a speech demanding that:

- there should be no co-operation with the Provisional Government
- the war should be ended immediately
- the land should be given to the peasants
- the Soviets should take power.

The points in Lenin's speech were later written up as the APRIL THESES, in which Lenin argued that there should be a second revolution – a Socialist revolution – in which the workers took power. Many Bolsheviks were surprised, and some did not take him seriously.

SOURCE 1   A 1930s painting of Lenin making a speech on his arrival at the Finland Station in Petrograd

The Bolshevik Party turned Lenin's ideas into the slogans 'Bread, Peace, Land' and 'All Power to the Soviets'. This was what the people wanted to hear. Support for the Bolsheviks began to grow, although as you can see from Source 2 they were outnumbered in the Soviets by other Socialists.

SOURCE 2   In June 1917 all the Soviets in Russia selected representatives to go to the First All-Russian Congress of Soviets. These were the results

Socialist Revolutionaries	285
Mensheviks	248
Bolsheviks	105
Other Socialists	105

July Days

The war was the big issue that distinguished the Bolsheviks from other groups. Only they opposed the war.

Over the summer of 1917, the ordinary people became more and more opposed to the war as shortages continued. Matters came to a head in July, when Kerensky launched a major attack on the Germans. This turned out to be a huge mistake, leading to a terrible defeat. It sparked an enormous demonstration in Petrograd, which became known as the 'July Days'. Soldiers, sailors and workers poured onto the streets on 16 and 17 July to protest about the war. Naturally, they turned to the Bolsheviks, the anti-war party, to lead them. But the Bolsheviks were not ready to seize power.

The demonstrations turned to rioting, and eventually troops were sent in to break up the mobs. Kerensky used this opportunity to produce evidence – letters – that seemed to show that Lenin was in the pay of the Germans. Lenin fled to Finland, and other leading Bolsheviks were arrested. It seemed that the Bolsheviks had missed their opportunity. Kerensky became Prime Minister.

SOURCE 3 Troops fire on demonstrators during the July Days

Autumn 1917 – a second chance

Fortunately for the Bolsheviks, events now started to work in their favour. Kerensky had appointed a general called Kornilov to be head of the army. But Kornilov decided that it was time to deal with the revolutionaries once and for all and to establish strong government in Russia – his own government. He ordered his Cossack troops to march on Petrograd.

The people in Petrograd panicked; there was bound to be violence and bloodshed. Kerensky also panicked and asked the Bolsheviks for help. He gave rifles to the Bolshevik Red Guard, groups of workers who had been training secretly, and who now appeared on the streets to help defend the city. But Kornilov's troops never arrived. The railway workers stopped the trains carrying the troops, and workers and other soldiers persuaded them not to fight their fellow Russians. However, the Red Guard kept their rifles.

SOURCE 4 Lenin had to shave off his beard to escape. Any films or photographs of Lenin during this time which show Lenin with a beard are fakes, usually produced well after the Revolution

The time is right

The Bolsheviks were now the 'saviours' of Petrograd, and their support was at an all-time high. They won an overall majority in elections to the Petrograd Soviet and Leon Trotsky, a recent recruit to the Bolsheviks, was elected chairman.

Meanwhile, the situation in the rest of Russia was deteriorating fast. In the countryside, the peasants were seizing land at an increased rate. Kerensky sent out punishment brigades to try to stop the land seizures, but this only made the peasants hate the Provisional Government more. Soldiers were deserting from the army in their thousands, trying to get back to their villages to get a share of the land. Food was rationed in the cities and prices were rising fast. It began to get cold as winter approached.

From his hiding place in Finland, Lenin sent messages to the Bolsheviks telling them to seize power now that they controlled the Soviets. But leading Bolsheviks refused to carry out his instructions. So Lenin returned to Petrograd in disguise. He spent the night of 23 October arguing with them until they gave in. He wanted them to seize power straight away, but Trotsky persuaded him to wait.

SOURCE 5 The situation at the end of the summer, reported by an eye-witness, N. Sukanov

Lynch law, the destruction of homes and shops, jeering at and attacks on officers, unauthorised arrests, seizures and beatings up were recorded every day by tens and hundreds. In the country, burnings and destruction of country houses became more frequent.

Military discipline collapsed . . . There were masses of deserters. The soldiers, without leave, went off home in great floods. They filled all the trains, kicked out the passengers and threatened the entire transport system.

■ TASK

You have been chosen by the Bolsheviks to report on the general situation in Russia in October 1917 to see if various groups are likely to support you if you try to seize power. You are particularly interested in:

■ the state of mind of the soldiers and their morale
■ the attitude of the peasants
■ the conditions of the workers in Petrograd.

Use Sources 5–7 and the other information in this section to help you make your report.

SOURCE 6 Bread rations per person per day in Petrograd in 1917

	March	April	September	October
Manual workers	675g	335g	225g	110g
Others	450g	335g	225g	110g

SOURCE 7 John Reed, an American journalist, describes Petrograd in *Ten Days that Shook the World*

September and October are the worst months of the Russian year – especially the Petrograd year. Under dull grey skies, in the shortening days, the rain fell drenching, incessant . . .

It was dark from three in the afternoon till ten in the morning. Robberies and housebreaking increased. In the apartment houses the men took turns at all-night guard duty, armed with loaded rifles.

Week by week, food became scarcer. The daily allowance of bread fell . . . Towards the end there was a week without bread at all. Sugar one was entitled to at the rate of two pounds per month – if one could get it at all, which was seldom. A bar of chocolate cost anywhere from seven to ten roubles – at least a dollar. There was milk for half the babies in the city; most hotels and private houses never saw it for months. For milk and tobacco one had to stand in a queue long hours in the chill rain.

SOURCE 8 Bolsheviks distributing leaflets

The Bolsheviks seize power

The Bolsheviks had their headquarters in the Smolny Institute, a former girls' school. It was from here that Trotsky organised the takeover of the city, planned for 7 November. It was no secret – the newspapers carried articles about it and the Bolsheviks distributed leaflets saying it was going to happen. Kerensky, dosing himself on brandy and morphine, desperately rushed round the city trying to find troops to help him.

Trotsky made his first moves in the early hours of 7 November. As the city slept, small groups of Bolshevik Red Guards moved out. Lenin and Trotsky were gloomy, realising that they were finished if Kerensky could get enough troops together. The Red Guards took control of the bridges, the main telegraph office, the railway stations and the power stations. In most cases, other troops just melted away as the Red Guards arrived.

During the morning of the next day, the Bolsheviks carried on seizing key places, such as the State Bank. But otherwise all seemed normal. The shops and factories were open and the trams were running. Nobody seemed to be taking much notice, and many people thought the Bolsheviks would be defeated as soon as Kerensky arrived with troops. But Kerensky had left the city in a car lent by the American Embassy and did not return.

SOURCE 9   Bolsheviks outside the Smolny Institute

SOURCE 10   A map of Petrograd, showing the key points taken over by the Bolsheviks

Finland Station

VYBORG DISTRICT

PETROGRAD SIDE

Tauride Palace (Headquarters of the Soviet)

Fortress of St Peter and St Paul

Palace Bridge

Winter Palace

VASILEVSKY ISLAND

Nevsky Prospekt

Smolny Institute (Bolshevik Headquarters)

Gulf Of Finland

Nikolaevsky Bridge

Sadovaya St.

Fontanka Canal

Moscow Station

Neva River

Moika Canal

Catherine Canal

Baltic Station

Warsaw Station

0   3 km

Storming the Winter Palace

The Bolsheviks now moved in on the Winter Palace, where the Provisional Government was meeting. But morale among the defenders of the Winter Palace was very low. During the afternoon, most of the Cossacks had slipped out of the palace, leaving some military cadets and the Women's Death Battalion.

At 9.00 p.m. the *Aurora* (a ship whose sailors supported the Bolsheviks) fired a blank shot to start the attack. There was a little machine-gun fire, but very little damage was done to the Palace. The Women's Death Battalion offered no resistance, came out and went back to camp. The Red Guards entered and made their way along the miles of corridors. When they did meet military cadets, they gave up, as did the Provisional Government when the Red Guards found them. The Bolsheviks had control of Petrograd.

1. Looking at the map, Source 10, explain why the bridges were particularly important.
2. Why did the Bolsheviks seize the railway stations and telephone exchange on the first night?
3. How was the storming of the Winter Palace represented by the Bolsheviks in paintings like Source 11 and street theatre events like that shown in Source 12?
4. How does this compare with what happened?
5. How useful are these sources as evidence?

SOURCE 11 (above)   A painting made in Russia in the 1930s by Sokolov-Skalya, showing the storming of the Winter Palace

SOURCE 12   One of the street theatre events staged in the years after the Revolution, celebrating the storming of the Winter Palace. This photograph is often used to portray the actual storming

■ ACTIVITY

You have been working in the British Embassy in Petrograd throughout 1917. The British Government have asked you to tell them how Lenin has been able to seize control. You talk to your colleagues, who have different views.

Use these views to help you write your report explaining how the Bolsheviks were able to seize power. At the end, you should describe what happened on the day of the Revolution. Ask your teacher for a worksheet to help you.

The Provisional Government made mistakes. It did not end the war and it did not give the land to the peasants. If it had done these things, it would have got the people on its side.

No, it was the war. Even after the Tsar had gone, things did not get better. There was still no food and fuel because of the war. It was this that brought the people to desperation point. It also caused the collapse of the Russian army which would not support the Provisional Government.

The Provisional Government was to blame. It was weak and never had any real power.

I think it was more to do with the Bolsheviks and their leader Lenin. He knew what he wanted right from the beginning.

The Bolsheviks were very determined, it is true. They were the only ones who had a clear plan and were well organised. Everybody else was not sure what to do.

They certainly knew what the people wanted – bread, peace and land. They promised the land to the peasants and were the only group who wanted to end the war.

Mind you, they had some luck. That Kornilov fellow came along at the right moment – helped them no end.

Did Lenin make a difference?

■ SOURCE INVESTIGATION

WOULD THERE have been a revolution in November 1917 if Lenin had not returned to Russia? Look back over pages 38–47 and study the evidence below. What conclusions can you reach?

Now is the time for a Socialist revolution.

April 1917

THESIS

This isn't what Marx said.

Is he mad?

He must be wrong!

SOURCE 1   A painting of Lenin returning to Petrograd in April 1917, made in the USSR in the 1930s. Trotsky called Lenin the 'engine driver of the Revolution'

SOURCE 2   From V. Serge's book *From Lenin to Stalin*, 1937. Serge was a Bolshevik supporter in Petrograd in 1917

66 *Hardly off the train, Lenin asked the Party comrades, 'Why didn't you seize power?' And at once he comes out with his April Theses . . . He is called mad and delirious . . . But suddenly it becomes apparent that he has the ear of the man in the street, and of the man in the factory and barracks! His whole genius consists in his ability to say what these people want to say, but do not know how to say.* 99

SOURCE 3   Sukanov, a non-Bolshevik Socialist journalist describes reactions to Lenin's speech on his return to Russia in April 1917

66 *Dear Comrades, soldiers, sailors and workers! [said Lenin]. I am happy to greet in your persons the victorious Russian Revolution, and greet you as vanguard [leaders] of the worldwide proletarian army . . . Long live the worldwide Socialist revolution!'*
. . . Suddenly, before the eyes of all of us, completely swallowed up by the routine drudgery of the Revolution, there was presented a bright, blinding, exotic beacon . . . Lenin's voice heard straight from the train, was a 'voice from outside'. 99

Look back at page 42 before answering these two questions.

1. What, according to Sources 2 and 3, was Lenin saying that was so different?
2. Why did Lenin's arrival have such an impact on the Bolshevik Party and the workers and soldiers?

There was an argument between Lenin and other Bolshevik leaders about whether they should seize power at the end of October. Lenin sent a letter to the Bolshevik Central Committee, written on 6 October from his hiding place in Finland.

SOURCE 4

Having obtained the majority in the Soviet of Workers' and Soldiers' Deputies in both capitals, the Bolsheviks can and must take state power into their hands.

But when the Committee met, Lenin's proposal was defeated by 4 votes to 6 with 6 abstaining. On 23 October, Lenin returned secretly to Petrograd and persuaded the Bolshevik Central Committee to agree to his plans. He talked to them through the entire night until they gave in. However, Trotsky persuaded Lenin to wait until 7 November. The next day, Zinoviev and Kamenev, leading Bolsheviks, sent a letter to the Bolshevik Party opposing the uprising.

To call at present for an armed uprising means to stake on one card not only the fate of our party, but also the fate of the Russian and international revolution . . . A majority of workers and a significant part of the army in Russia is for us. But all the rest are in question. We are convinced [that] . . . the majority of peasants will vote for the Socialist Revolutionaries . . . If we take power now and are forced to wage a revolutionary war, the mass of the soldiers will not support us.

Lenin had to continue to urge leading Bolsheviks to be active in supporting the seizure of power. He sent this letter to the other Bolshevik leaders on the evening before the Revolution.

The situation is extremely critical. Delaying the uprising now really means death . . . We must at any price, tonight, arrest the Ministers, having disarmed the military cadets, etc.

We must not wait! We may lose everything! . . . The government is tottering. We must deal it the death blow at any cost.

What do historians say?

SOURCE 5   From *1917, the Russian Revolutions* by Leonard Schapiro

In the actual organisation of the final stages of the Bolshevik Revolution, Lenin's role fell far short of Trotsky's . . . Yet there is no doubt that without Lenin the Bolshevik coup would have been postponed and might have failed . . .

SOURCE 6   From *The Russian Revolution*, by Robert Service, 1986

He had limitless capacity to persuade, cajole and goad. On 23 October, the Central Committee debated the question of state power. Lenin returned clandestinely [secretly] from Finland to participate, and the consequent decision came from his pen. Still he had to be restrained. He wanted power seized immediately. Trotsky's view was preferred, that the uprising would be . . . on the opening day of the Second All-Russian Congress of Soviets.

SOURCE 7   A view of Lenin by a Soviet writer, Y. Kukushkin, in *History of the USSR*, published in the USSR in 1981

The Bolshevik party was waging a determined struggle to win over the masses. The struggle was headed by Lenin, who led and guided the Party's Central Committee . . . He frequently addressed mass rallies and meetings. Lenin's speeches, noted for their profound content and brilliant delivery, inspired workers and soldiers . . . The Bolshevik Party's membership began to grow rapidly.

3. Does Source 4 show that it was mainly Lenin who was pushing the Bolsheviks to seize power? Explain your answer by referring to different parts of Source 4.
4. Why did Zinoviev and Kamenev not want to seize power in October?
5. Write a paragraph summing up what Sources 2–4 tell us about Lenin's role in 1917.
6. a) Do the historians in Sources 5, 6 and 7 support this view?
   b) What else do they tell us?
7. Do you think that one man – Lenin – really made a difference in 1917?

chapter 5

HOW DID THE BOLSHEVIKS KEEP POWER AFTER 1917?

How did the Bolsheviks stay in power?

LENIN HAD SEIZED power in Petrograd, but for how long could he hold on to it? A few days after the takeover, Kerensky sent troops to put the Provisional Government back in control, but they were easily stopped in the suburbs by a force of pro-Bolshevik workers, soldiers and sailors. In Moscow, the fighting was fiercer. Other cities also came out in favour of the Bolsheviks, but they controlled only a small area of Russia.

Meanwhile, Lenin set up his government, called the Sovnakom – the 'Council of People's Commissars'. Lenin was chairman, Trotsky was Commissar for War and Stalin was Commissar for Nationalities. There was only one woman in the Sovnakom – Alexandra Kollontai.

Lenin pushed ahead with his first measures. It was important that he carry out his promises: to end the war, to give land to the peasants and to get food to the cities. Otherwise, his support would disappear.

The first months

Decrees made by the Sovnakom in the first few months of power

November
- A maximum eight-hour day and 48-hour week declared for industrial workers
- Employment insurance introduced for workers for injuries, illness and unemployment
- All titles and class distinctions abolished – no dukes or lords, the title 'comrade' for everybody
- Women declared equal to men
- All non-Bolshevik newspapers banned

December
- Liberal party, the Cadets, banned
- All factories to be put under the control of workers' committees
- All banks taken over by the government
- The army to be more democratic – officers to be elected, no ranks or saluting
- Church land to be confiscated by the state
- Divorce made easier and marriages do not have to be in churches

SOURCE 1 A collage of photographs showing members of Lenin's new government

Land
In November, a decree was passed taking all the land away from the Tsar and the old landlords. Land was to be given to the peasants, who would form committees to divide it up fairly.

Food
Lenin put an absolute priority on getting food to the cities. Where peasants would not sell their produce, he sent out the police and the Cheka to take it.

The Cheka

In December 1917, Lenin set up the Cheka. The head of this secret police force was the cold and incorruptible Felix Dzerzhinski. He set up headquarters in the 'Lubyanka' in Moscow, a name that was to become feared because of the torture and executions that were carried out there.

The Cheka arrested people who were considered dangerous. After an assassination attempt on Lenin, the Cheka launched the Red Terror. Anybody who spoke out against the government was arrested, and many were shot without trial. Sometimes it was enough to be someone who might oppose the Bolsheviks. The use of terror to control people was to become a feature of the new regime.

Constituent Assembly

Lenin had been forced, in November 1917, into holding the elections promised by the Provisional Government. The railway workers said that they would shut down the railways if Lenin did not go ahead with Russia's first free elections. These were to choose a Constituent Assembly, which would work out how Russia would be governed in the future.

This was a real threat to Lenin, as the party with most votes would probably form a new government. The results of the elections can be seen in Source 2. Shortly after the Constituent Assembly met in January 1918, Lenin sent in soldiers to shut it down for good.

SOURCE 2 The results of the November 1917 election

Party	Seats in Constituent Assembly
Socialist Revolutionaries	370
Bolsheviks	175
Left Socialist Revolutionaries (supporters of Bolsheviks)	40
Cadets	17
Mensheviks	16
Others	89

A new name
In 1918, Lenin changed the name of the Bolshevik Party. They were now called COMMUNISTS.

Peace

Lenin sent Trotsky to meet the Germans to negotiate a peace treaty. Trotsky walked out of the talks because the Germans demanded so much territory. He said there would be 'no peace, no war'. However, Lenin sent him back, because he was sure that the Bolsheviks would stay in power only if the war could be ended quickly. The result was the harsh Treaty of Brest-Litovsk in March 1918.

Key

Land lost in Treaty of Brest-Litovsk
Russia lost:
- 62 million people (one-sixth of the population)
- 27 per cent of farm land (some of the best in Russia)
- 26 per cent of railways
- 74 per cent of iron ore and coal

SOURCE 3 A map showing land lost in the Treaty of Brest-Litovsk

■ TASK

1. Consider the following people. Decide which of Lenin's actions described on pages 50–51 would have been popular with each person and which would not. You could do this in the form of a chart, with the names of the people along the top and the different actions down the side. (Your teacher will give you a sheet to fill in.)

   ■ woman worker
   ■ Tsarist army officer
   ■ industrialist
   ■ Socialist Revolutionary
   ■ peasant
   ■ middle-class liberal
   ■ soldier

2. a) Which of the actions mentioned would have increased support for Lenin?
   b) Which do you think would have been most unpopular amongst different groups of people?
3. Had Lenin honoured his promises?
4. Which political party had been elected to form the new government of Russia?
5. How did Lenin deal with opposition and threats to his power?

How did the Communists win the Civil War?

BY THE SUMMER of 1918, the Communists (the new name for the Bolsheviks) found themselves under attack. They only controlled a small part of Russia and their enemies were determined that they should not remain in power for long. This was the beginning of a vicious civil war which was to tear Russia apart.

There were three main sides:

The Reds: the Bolsheviks or Communists (red was the colour of Communism).

The Whites: all the opponents of the Bolsheviks – tsarists and nobles, middle-class constitutional democrats, Mensheviks and Socialist Revolutionaries. The Whites got their name from the white uniforms worn by tsarist officers. This meant that the Whites were always associated with the Tsar and the old system of government.

The Greens: independent groups of nationalists, peasants or bandits who roamed Russia at this time. They fought anyone and raided villages and towns. The most famous was the Ukrainian nationalist, Nestor Makno, who shared his booty with local peasants.

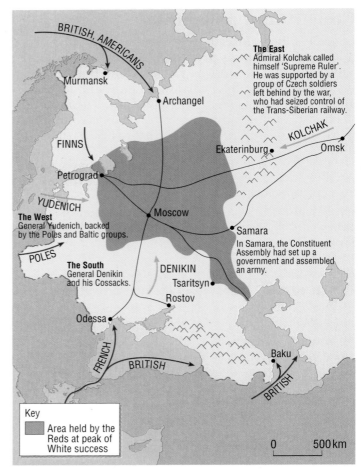

The East
Admiral Kolchak called himself 'Supreme Ruler'. He was supported by a group of Czech soldiers left behind by the war, who had seized control of the Trans-Siberian railway.

The West
General Yudenich, backed by the Poles and Baltic groups.

The South
General Denikin and his Cossacks.

In Samara, the Constituent Assembly had set up a government and assembled an army.

Key
▨ Area held by the Reds at peak of White success

0   500 km

SOURCE 1   A map showing the events of the Civil War

But the real struggle was between the Reds and the Whites. The Greens were fighting for themselves, not for control of Russia. A number of factors played a crucial role in the war. These included the aims of both sides, geographical factors, leadership and unity, and foreign intervention.

Geographical factors

Reds	Whites
■ They held the central area of western Russia, which contained most of the large industrial centres able to produce munitions and war supplies. ■ They had control of the railway lines which connected Petrograd and Moscow to the rest of the country. This meant that they could send soldiers and munitions quickly to any place in the battle area.	■ They were scattered around this central area, often with hundreds of miles separating the different armies. ■ Communications were difficult – that is, if the generals wanted to communicate.

Aims

Reds	Whites
■ They had only one aim: to stay in power so that they could build the new Socialist society.	■ The groups which made up the Whites had different aims: some wanted the Tsar back, some a military DICTATOR; others wanted constitutional government or revolutionary change. The only aim they had in common was to defeat the Bolsheviks; they agreed on little else.

Leadership and unity

Reds	Whites
■ They had a superb leader in Trotsky. He built up the Red Army from nothing, introducing conscription for men over eighteen years of age. He brought in nearly 50,000 experienced former Tsarist officers and appointed political Commissars – fanatical Bolsheviks – to each unit of men to make sure the officers and soldiers carried out their orders. ■ Trotsky was personally very courageous. He had a special train which took him and his army of hand-picked soldiers to the places where the fighting was hardest.	■ They lacked good leaders. Often the commanders were cruel, treated their men with disrespect and set a bad example, drinking and taking drugs. ■ The White generals did not trust each other and would not co-ordinate their attacks. This allowed the Reds to pick off the White armies one by one. ■ The Whites had problems inside their armies, too. There was often fighting and squabbling, because groups had different aims and beliefs. It was particularly hard for revolutionaries to co-operate with supporters of the Tsar.

Foreign intervention

The Whites had the advantage of support from foreign powers. Britain, France, Japan and the USA, along with several other countries, sent forces to help them. Their governments did not want to see Bolshevism spread into Europe. However, although the supplies and armaments they gave to the Whites were very valuable, their troops did not fight. They were tired of war, and some of the soldiers were sympathetic to the Bolshevik cause. There was a mutiny of the French navy in the Black Sea, and the British Labour Party protested at the use of British troops to crush Russian workers. The Americans were there only to make sure that the Japanese did not seize territory in the east. So the Allied intervention was half-hearted and ineffective.

The intervention of foreign countries helped the Communists. They portrayed the Whites as being used by foreign CAPITALIST powers, while they themselves were the defenders of ordinary Russian people from foreign invaders.

SOURCE 2   A Bolshevik poster. The names of the dogs are Denikin, Kolchak and Yudenich

1. Who is holding the leads of the dogs in Source 2?
2. What is the message of the cartoon?
3. How does Source 1 help us understand why the Reds won the Civil War?
4. What do you think was the main problem facing the Whites?

53

The War

By the end of 1918, the Civil War was not going well for the Reds. White forces were pressing in from all sides, and the Reds suffered a series of defeats. Trotsky worked hard to organise the Red Army.

Fortunately for him, the White armies did not attack together. This allowed him to move his forces to deal with one attack at a time.

It was in the middle of 1919 that the real test came. In the west, General Yudenich came within 30 miles of Petrograd, only to be turned back by determined resistance led by Trotsky's special forces. General Denikin was also very successful, advancing from the south to within 200 miles of Moscow. Much depended on Admiral Kolchak's attack from the east linking up with Denikin's forces. But Kolchak's army fell apart because different groups would not co-operate and started arguing and fighting with each other. The Socialist Revolutionaries in particular refused to fight with Kolchak.

The Red Army now attacked ferociously, and Denikin was pushed further and further back. In the east, Kolchak's forces disintegrated and he was shot. By 1920, the main White threat was over. The war

lingered on, particularly in a desperate battle with the Poles, but this was settled by the Treaty of Riga in 1921.

Fighting in the Civil War was bitter and cruel. Both sides were guilty of atrocities. At Rostov miners supporting the Bolsheviks were buried alive in their mines. At Kharkov, Bolsheviks nailed epaulets to White soldiers while the victims were still alive.

The war was also confusing. Units of soldiers often changed sides, sometimes several times. Some units shot their officers and went home. The fighting moved back and forth across the country: Kiev changed hands sixteen times. And the people suffered whichever side was in control of their area. Both Red and White units looted and raided villages, requisitioning (taking) grain and animals.

The role of the peasants in the Civil War was crucial. They made up most of the armies on both sides, and the side they supported was likely to win. In the end, the peasants were more willing to support the Reds, because the Reds said they could keep the land. The Whites, on the other hand, made it clear that they would restore the land to the old landlords.

SOURCE 3 A photograph of Trotsky and his special train. The arrival of Trotsky's special train would raise morale, but the soldiers also knew they would have to fight hard

SOURCE 4   A White colonel describes the punishment of a village accused of supporting the Reds, in March 1918

The mounted platoon entered the village, met the Bolshevik committee and put the members to death . . . After the execution, the houses of the culprits were burned and the whole male population under 45 whipped soundly . . . Then the population was ordered to deliver without pay the best cattle, pigs, fowl, forage and bread for the whole detachment, as well as the best horses. All this they kept bringing over until nightfall . . . The whole village set up a howl . . .

SOURCE 5   Isaac Babel was a volunteer in a revolutionary Cossack regiment. In his book *Red Cavalry* he wrote stories which reflected the savagery of the Civil War. This extract comes from a story he called 'A Letter', in which a family is split, with the father fighting on one side and his sons on the other

Dear Mother,
. . . I am alive and well . . . I hasten to describe to you about Dad, that he killed our brother Theodore a year ago. Our Red brigade was advancing on the town of Rostov. Dad was then with General Denikin (Whites), commanding a company . . . and they took us all prisoners . . . Dad noticed my brother Theodore. And Dad began cutting him about, saying, 'Brute, Red cur, son of a bitch,' and all sorts of other things, and went on cutting him about until dark and Theodore passed away . . .

I soon ran away from Dad and managed to get back to my unit . . . Then brother Simon and I began to pursue General Denikin, and killed thousands of them, and drove them into the Black Sea. Only Dad was nowhere to be seen. So Dear Mother, what d'you think Dad did? He had dyed his beard shamelessly from red to black and was staying in the town of Maykop in civvies . . .

But Simon got Dad all right and he began to whip Dad . . . and asked him:
'You all right, Dad, in my hands?'
'No,' says Dad, 'not all right.'
Then Simon said: 'And Theo, was he all right in your hands when you killed him?'
'No,' says Dad. 'Things went badly for Theo.' . . .

Then Simon turned to us all and said: 'And what I think is that if I got caught by his boys, there wouldn't be no quarter for me – and now, Dad, we're going to finish you off.'

SOURCE 6   A White poster, showing Bolsheviks seizing grain

1. How does Source 4 help explain why the peasants would not support the Whites?
2. Why would the Whites produce a poster like the one in Source 6?
3. What do Sources 4–6 reveal about the nature of the Civil War?
4. Which do you think is more reliable – Source 4 or Source 5?

■ ACTIVITY

1. Draw up a chart to compare the advantages and disadvantages of the Reds and the Whites, using the headings below.

	Reds	Whites
Aims		
Geographical factors		
Leadership		
Unity		
Foreign intervention		
Peasant support		

2. Write a short essay explaining why the Reds won the Civil War. Use the headings in the chart as the key ideas for your paragraphs. You will find more useful information in the two investigations on pages 56–57 on a) the use of propaganda by the Reds; and b) the role of Trotsky.

How did the Communists use propaganda?

■ **SOURCE INVESTIGATION**

DURING THE period of the Civil War, the Communists produced over 3,000 political posters. Some of these used exciting new avant-garde designs, which became popular in Russia after the Revolution.

SOURCE 1 (right) 'Shoulder to shoulder in the defence of Petrograd'. This poster was used when Petrograd was under threat in 1919

1. Who are the people standing 'shoulder to shoulder'?
2. Why is this effective?

ЦАРСКИЕ ПОЛКИ И КРАСНАЯ АРМИЯ

SOURCE 2 (left) A Civil War poster showing Russia before and after the Revolution

3. What were the soldiers fighting for before the Revolution?
4. What were the forces fighting for after the Revolution?

SOURCE 3 (below) 'Drive Red wedges into White troops!' A poster by El Lissitzky, 1920

5. What is the 'Red wedge'?

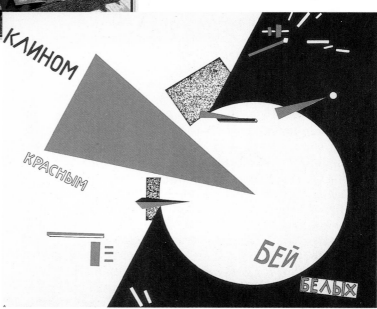

■ **TASK**

1. Imagine that you work in a museum and have to give a talk to a group of students using the posters on this page and the one on page 37. Explain:
   ■ the meaning of the posters, one by one
   ■ the different design styles
   ■ how effectively they put their messages across
   ■ which one you think is most effective and why.
2. Are these posters good evidence to show us what ordinary Russians were thinking during this period? If not, are they at all useful to historians?

How important was the role of Trotsky?

SOURCE 1 A photograph of Trotsky addressing the troops. He said, 'I issue this warning. If any detachment retreats without orders, the first to be shot will be the Commissar, the second the commander'

SOURCE 2 Orders to the Red Army from Trotsky, 1918

> ■ *Every scoundrel who incites anyone to retreat, to desert, or not to fulfil a military order, will be shot.*
> ■ *Every soldier of the Red Army who voluntarily deserts his post will be shot.*
> ■ *Every soldier who throws away his rifle or sells part of his equipment will be shot.*
> ■ *Those guilty of harbouring deserters are liable to be shot.*

SOURCE 3 From *Memoirs of a Revolutionary* by V. Serge

> *The news from the other fronts was so bad that Lenin was reluctant to sacrifice the last available forces in the defence of the doomed city [Petrograd]. Trotsky thought otherwise ... He arrived at almost the last moment and his presence changed the atmosphere ...*
>
> *Trotsky arrived with a train, that famous train which had been speeding to and fro along the different fronts ... The train contained excellent motor cars ... a printing shop for propaganda, sanitary squads, and specialists in engineering, provisioning, street fighting, all bound together by friendship and trust, all kept to a strict, vigorous discipline by a leader they admired, all dressed in black leather, red stars on their peaked caps, all exhaling energy. It was a nucleus of resolute and efficiently serviced organisers, who hastened wherever danger demanded their presence.*

SOURCE 4 Trotsky's comment on Bolshevik doubts about using former Tsarist officers in the Red Army

> *[Political] Commissars [attached to each army unit] were required to keep a record of the families of officers and would admit them to posts of authority provided it was possible in the event of betrayal to detain the family in question.*

SOURCE 5 Trotsky describes how he built up the Red Army

> *The flabby, panicky mob would be transformed in two or three weeks into an efficient fighting force. What was needed for this? It needed good commanders, a few dozen experienced fighters, a dozen or so of Communists ready to make any sacrifice, boots for the barefooted, a bath-house, an energetic propaganda campaign, food, underwear, tobacco and matches. The train took care of all this.*

1. Use Sources 1–5 and the section on leadership (Reds) on page 53 to explain why Trotsky's role in the Civil War was so important.

What happened to the Tsar and his family?

■ SOURCE INVESTIGATION

AFTER HIS abdication in March 1917, the Tsar and his family were held under house arrest just outside St Petersburg. For their safety, they were sent to Tobolsk in Siberia. Later they were moved to Ekaterinburg in the Urals, where they were held by the Reds (Bolsheviks) in the house of a family called Ipatiev.

The Tsar presented a continuing problem for the Reds. If he escaped, he might help unite the White forces; if executed, he could become a martyr. But when White forces closed in on Ekaterinburg in the summer of 1918, it seems that the decision was taken to kill him.

According to one account, the family were awoken during the night of 17 July. They were told that there was trouble in the town and that they would be safer downstairs. They dressed quickly and the Tsar carried his sick son down to a basement room where they were told to wait. With the Tsar was his wife, Alexandra, his son and four daughters, the family doctor and three servants (eleven people in all). Yakov Yurovsky led a group of twelve soldiers into the now crowded room. Yurovsky announced that the Tsar was to be executed and, before the Tsar could protest, opened fire. Nicholas and Alexandra died quickly but the girls, who had jewels sewn into their clothing which deflected the bullets, had to be finished off with bayonets.

But is this the true story of what took place? Who exactly was shot and what happened to the bodies? This was the beginning of a history mystery which has gone on for most of the twentieth century. A number of people have turned up claiming to be one of the Tsar's children, most famously a woman who claimed to be his daughter Anastasia.

SOURCE 1 The death of the Tsar, painted by S. Sarmet, based on the investigation carried out by the Whites

Much of the evidence comes from two investigations carried out by the Whites after they had captured Ekaterinburg in late 1918:

■ Investigation 1 by Judge Sergeyev, who was removed from the investigation in 1919 and died shortly afterwards in mysterious circumstances.
■ Investigation 2 by Judge Sokolov. But before the investigation was completed, the Reds recaptured Ekaterinburg.

Examine the evidence for yourselves.

SOURCE 2 Interview with Pavel Medvedev, Red Guard commander. This is the only eye-witness account from 1919. It was later claimed that he had been tortured. Also, he gave himself up to the Whites in strange circumstances

66 *The sovereign walked ahead with the heir [Alexis]. In my presence there were no tears, no sobs, and no questions . . . The Empress sat down by the wall . . . behind her stood her three daughters. The Emperor was in the middle, next to the heir, and behind stood Dr Botkin. (Another daughter stood next to the maid.) . . . Eleven men walked into the room: Yurovsky, his assistant, the two from the Cheka, and seven Latvians.*

Medvedev said that he was sent out of the room to see if the shots could be heard. He heard the shots and returned to see the Tsar's family lying on the floor.

The blood was gushing . . . the heir was still alive – and moaning. Yurovsky walked over to him and shot him two or three times at point blank range . . . The scene made me want to vomit. 99

SOURCE 3   The room in Ipatiev house in which the execution took place

SOURCE 4   Judge Sergeyev, the first investigator, in an interview with the *New York Tribune* just before he was removed from the investigation in January 1919

I do not believe that all the . . . people, the Tsar, his family, and those with them, were shot there. It is my belief that the Empress, the Tsar's son and the four other children were not shot in that house. I believe, however, that the Tsar, the family doctor, two servants and the maid were shot in the Ipatiev house.

SOURCE 5   Sir Charles Eliot was sent by the British government to find out what happened to the Tsar and his family. In October 1918, Eliot talked to Judge Sergeyev who showed him the supposed murder room

On the wall, the door and on the floor were marks showing [bullet holes] . . . There is no real evidence as to who or how many the victims were . . . No corpses were discovered, nor any trace of their having been disposed of by burning or otherwise . . . The marks in the room prove at most that some persons unknown were shot there . . .

The Reds and the Whites both had good reasons for telling particular stories:

■ **The Reds** were holding vital peace talks with the Germans at Brest-Litovsk. If the Germans thought the Reds had killed the Tsarina and her children (with their connections to the German royal family) the talks might have failed – a disaster for Lenin.

■ **The Whites** could use the cruel murder of the whole family to get support. Many Russians and foreign governments would be horrified if the family were murdered.

SOURCE 6   Judge Sokolov, the second investigator, reported that all the Romanov family had been killed and that the bodies had been taken away for disposal

The bloody carnage took place in one of the rooms of the lower, basement, floor . . . The murder was perpetrated with revolvers and bayonets. More than thirty shots were fired . . . Several people were murdered . . .
On 17th July, under cover of darkness, a lorry carried their corpses to the Four Brothers mine . . . At the open shaft, the corpses were stripped. The clothing was crudely removed, torn away . . . The main purpose was to destroy the bodies. For this it was necessary, first of all, to cut them up. The dissected bodies were burned on bonfires with the aid of petrol and destroyed with sulphuric acid . . . the murderers threw [into the mineshaft] objects which had resisted the fire, or which in their haste, they had forgotten to destroy.

1. Taking each of Sources 1–7 in turn, explain:
   a) what type of source it is (eye-witness account, etc.)
   b) what it tells/shows us about the murder
   c) whether it is good/not good proof that the Tsar and his family were shot. Give reasons.
      You could set this out in three columns.
2. What crucial piece of evidence is missing?
3. Does the evidence prove that the Tsar and all his family were murdered?

SOURCE 7   Among items found in the mineshaft were Princess Tatiana's dog, a finger claimed to be the Tsarina's, and corsets (undamaged by bullets)

A different story

Other evidence collected during or after the White investigations seems to tell a different story. We must remember that:

a) this was a very confused time when communications often broke down and thousands of people disappeared
b) the Reds and Whites, and the other people involved in the events, had reasons for telling different stories
c) witnesses can be mistaken.

SOURCE 8 Announcement by the Bolsheviks (Reds) on 18 July

In recent days, the danger of approach of the Czechoslovak forces [Whites] posed a serious threat to Ekaterinburg . . . In view of these circumstances, the leaders of the Ural Soviet decided to shoot Nicholas Romanov, and this was carried out on 16 July. The wife and son of Nicholas have been sent to a safe place.

1. Use Sources 8–11 to complete a chart like the one below. Decide whether you think each of the statements is possibly true, likely, highly likely or certainly true.
2. Why might the Reds lie in their announcement in Source 8?
3. How helpful is Source 9 when supported by the other sources?
4. What is the problem with the eye-witness reports in Sources 10 and 11?

■ ACTIVITY

a) Write a different version of the story to that given on pages 58 and 59. Include evidence that supports your new version.
b) Explain why the evidence about the death of the Tsar and his family is so confusing.

SOURCE 9 From Sir Charles Eliot's report

On 17 July a train with the blinds down left Ekaterinburg for an unknown destination and it is believed that the surviving members of the imperial family were in it.

SOURCE 10 The eye-witness account of a nurse, Natalya Mutnykh, in March 1919

I found out by chance that the family of Nicholas II – his wife and four daughters – were transferred from the town of Ekaterinburg to Perm . . . [they] were kept very secretly . . . I was interested . . . and made use of the fact that my brother had to go on duty at the place where the imperial family were being kept, and asked him to take me with him . . . This was in September [1918] . . . We went down to the basement and I saw the room where in the poor candle-light I could make out the former Empress Alexandra and her four daughters, who were in a terrible state but I recognised them only too well.

Other eye-witnesses also claimed to have seen the Tsarina and her daughters in Perm four months after they were supposed to have been shot.

SOURCE 11 Testimony of Dr Utkin, February 1919. The doctor was called by the Cheka (the Red secret police) to treat a young woman who appeared to have been beaten up and possibly raped

. . . a young woman was lying semi-conscious, on a bed. She was plump and her dark brown hair had been cropped close . . . When I asked the sick woman 'Who are you?' she raised her head and said in a distressed voice: 'I am the sovereign's daughter, Anastasia.'

Another eye-witness mentioned an escape attempt by Anastasia.

	Possibly true	Likely	Highly likely	Certainly true
The Tsar and the whole family were shot.				
The Tsar and one or two others were shot.				
The Tsarina and her daughters were not shot.				
One or two of the daughters escaped.				

The final proof?

SOURCE 12 From *The Sunday Times*, 11 December 1994

Tsar's head recreated

Burial pit skull reconstructions show Anastasia was there

These are the faces that reveal the fate of the Russian imperial family, helping to end one of the century's mysteries. Reconstructions from the skulls of Tsar Nicholas II and his entourage show that Anastasia, the grand duchess many believed escaped the Bolsheviks, was indeed murdered in 1918.

Two of the imperial family's five children were missing when archaeologists opened a shallow burial pit in Ekaterinburg, 850 miles east of Moscow, in 1991. One was Alexei, the heir to the throne. The other missing child was a girl, prompting fierce speculation that Anastasia had survived, exactly as a number of pretenders claimed.

To make these faces possible, Russian forensic scientists spent four months piecing together skull fragments. Last week Vladimir Solovyov, the public prosecutor who will report on the fate of the Tsar and his family, said there was no doubt of the results.

'Now there is a clear answer,' he said. 'Anastasia is in the grave. There is no sign of Alexei or Maria.'

Rebuilding the imperial faces, using techniques sometimes employed in criminal inquiries in Britain, was difficult. Some skulls had been badly damaged by rifle butts during the execution, and by attempts to destroy all trace of the bodies with grenades and sulphuric acid.

Solovyov said the resulting faces, along with DNA tests and dental records, positively identify Nicholas II, his wife Alexandra and their daughters Olga, Tatiana and Anastasia.

His final report will confirm contemporary accounts of the execution. Marks on the skeletons show that the girls, protected by 'bullet-proof vests' of jewels sewn into their underclothes, had to be finished off by bayonets. The bodies were driven to an abandoned mine 20 miles away. 'They were thrown in, followed by several grenades,' Solovyov said. 'It was assumed that the blast would make the mine collapse but it didn't. The next day the bodies were put back on the lorry.'

Fate intervened again to hinder efforts to hide the evidence: the lorry became bogged down in a swamp. So the remains were buried right there.

Experts are now searching for the charred remains of Alexei and Maria – a find that really would end the story.

SOURCE 13 The contents of the burial pit

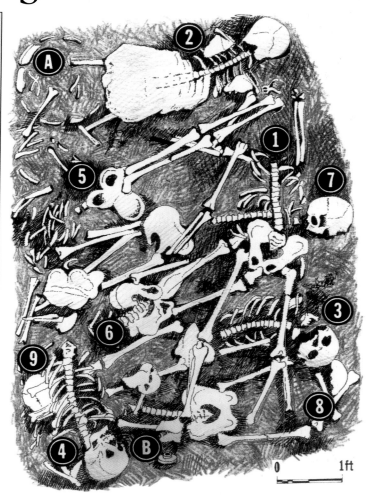

0 ___ 1ft

A and **B** The remnants of the crushed acid jars
1 The bones of Nicholas II; his skull was detached
2 Dr Botkin; his dentures were found elsewhere
3, 4, 6 Grand duchesses, bayonet marks on bones
5 and **9** Male servants; one still bound with rope
7 Alexandra
8 The worst damaged skeleton, Demidova the maid

5. Look at Sources 12 and 13.
a) Which version of the death of the Tsar and his family do these sources agree with?
b) What evidence do they provide?
c) Can we trust this evidence?
6. Could some of the stories about the Tsar's children escaping still be true?
7. What are your final conclusions about the death of Nicholas II and his family?

Discussion

What does this whole enquiry tell us about:

a) the problems of finding out what happened in history when there are gaps in evidence and conflicting evidence?
b) how new evidence can help fill out the picture?

Did the Tsar deserve to be shot?

War Communism

LENIN'S JOB during the Civil War was to run the government and to organise food and industrial production in the Red-held area. This was no easy task; food riots rocked several cities in spring 1918 and industry began to collapse as starving workers left the cities. However, it was crucial to keep the Red Army supplied. To do this, Lenin adopted a tough policy called 'War Communism'.

. . . in the towns

The state took control of industry, and told factories what to produce. The factories had been handed over to the control of workers' committees in 1917, but the committees did not run them very well. So Lenin now put in his own managers, and strict discipline was imposed on the workers. One report said: 'One might have thought that these were not factories but the forced labour prisons of Tsarist times.' Trade unions were not allowed, and workers were prevented from leaving the cities.

Food was rationed, but people could only get a ration card if they were working. The bread ration was sometimes as low as 200 grams a day. Larger rations were given to factory workers and soldiers. The only other way of getting food was through the illegal Black Market.

Money became virtually worthless (the rouble of 1920 was worth one per cent of its 1917 value). By 1920, wages were often paid in food or other goods, and many people bartered goods instead of using money.

. . . in the countryside

Lenin desperately needed food to feed the workers. Since the peasants were unwilling to sell their grain for money which had no value, he sent out units of the Cheka to seize surplus food. Those found hoarding supplies were punished harshly. The peasants resisted, and this became a bitter struggle. Many peasants decided to produce less grain, because they thought it would simply be taken away. So the situation got worse.

Terror

Over all this was the shadow of the Red Terror. The Cheka became increasingly brutal. People opposing the government were arrested and shot without trial or sent to labour camps. Many workers and peasants began to think that the workers' state was worse than the government of the Tsar which they had been so pleased to get rid of.

SOURCE 1 A unit of the Cheka marching in Rostov-on-Don on May Day 1920

SOURCE 2 An eye-witness account of the Black Market

❝The Black Market sells everything. There the former rich are selling their last items. The best grand piano sells for half the price of an ordinary record player . . . The formerly richest and most spoiled are now satisfied if they get some black bread and potatoes each day. An acquaintance of mine, formerly owner of a palace in Moscow, was given, as his place of residence, the bathroom of his former home. ❞

SOURCE 3 Many middle-class people, unable to get jobs or rations, sold their belongings to survive. Many nobles and middle-class Russians fled abroad to cities like Paris and New York, some ending up in menial jobs as waiters or doormen in hotels

SOURCE 4 From V. Serge's *Memoirs of a Revolutionary*

" Inside Petrograd's grand apartments people were crowded in one room, living around a little stove of brick or cast iron . . . Fuel for it would come from the floor boards nearby, from the last stick of furniture available, or else from books. Entire libraries disappeared in this way. "

SOURCE 5 From Arthur Ransome, *Six Weeks in Russia in 1919*. The wealthy were forced to share their houses with ordinary people, as Ransome describes

" Rooms are distributed on much the same plan as clothes. In every district there are housing committees to whom people wanting rooms apply. They work on the rough and ready theory that until every man has one room no-one has a right to two . . . This plan has, of course, proved very hard on house-owners, and in some cases the new tenants have made a horrible mess of the houses. "

SOURCE 6 Grain requisitioning

SOURCE 7 From V. Serge's *Memoirs of a Revolutionary*

" Parties which were sent into the countryside to obtain grain by requisition might be driven away by the peasants with pitchforks. Savage peasants would slit open a Commissar's belly, pack it with grain, and leave him by the roadside as a lesson to all. "

1. What were the key features of War Communism
 a) in the towns
 b) in the countryside?
2. What happened to many middle-class Russians (Sources 2, 3 and 5)?
3. Why do you think they found it so hard to get food?
4. Why did the struggle between the peasants and the requisition parties become so bitter?

SOURCE 8 P.D. Ouspensky, a writer, fled to southern Russia, where the situation was not much better, in 1919

" The price of all products and necessities has risen by 20, 50, 100 or 600 times. Workmen's wages have risen 20, 50 or even 100 times. But the salary of an ordinary 'brain-worker' – teacher, journalist or doctor – has risen in the best cases no more than three times . . .

I personally am still alive because my boots and trousers and other articles of clothing are still holding together. When they end their existence, I shall evidently end mine . . .

The prices are different in every place. To carry something from one town to another is to make money . . . 'the masses' rush to take part in the general looting . . . For a bag of flour or of bread, a basket of eggs or a jar of butter may bring them a fortune as reckoned in old values. So the trains and stations are crowded with people with bags and baskets; they carry typhus and cholera . . . "

■ **ACTIVITY**

Use Sources 1–8 to either

a) write a description of what life was like under War Communism; or
b) write a letter to middle-class relatives in America who fled Russia after the Bolsheviks seized power in 1917. Tell them:

■ how War Communism operates
■ how people in the cities are faring, particularly the middle classes
■ what is happening in the countryside
■ about the power of the Cheka and how control is kept.

1921 – a year of crisis

The results of War Communism

BY 1921, the economy of Russia was in ruins. Industrial production had fallen disastrously under War Communism. The cities were in chaos: gangs of orphaned children roamed the streets, robbery and burglary were common, stolen goods appeared on the thieves' markets. 'Bagmen' rode the trains, bringing supplies to the cities for a quick, if illegal, profit.

Agriculture had also collapsed. The disruption of the war and grain requisitioning had led to low grain harvests. Peasants saw little point in growing food. In 1921, even less grain was grown, because of a drought: this led to a horrendous famine, which killed up to five million people. A massive international aid operation was mounted, in which the USA played a major role.

SOURCE 1 Production of grain

1913: *80 million tons*   **1921:** *37.6 million tons*

SOURCE 2 Industrial output (in millions of tons)

	1913	1921
Coal	29	9
Oil	9.2	3.8
Iron	4.2	0.1
Steel	4.3	0.2
Sugar	1.3	0.05
Electricity (in million kWh)	2039	520

SOURCE 3 (left)   A peasant family during the famine

SOURCE 4   The famine affected both the countryside and the cities. There were reports of cannibalism in some districts. This was written in 1922

"Sometimes mothers and fathers feed their children human meat as a last resort. Sometimes a starving family eats the body of one of its junior members . . . Sometimes parents at night seize part of a body from a cemetery and feed it to their children."

SOURCE 5   Ludmilla Shapiro, an eye-witness, describes Moscow during the famine of 1921

"You could often see people who had walked from the famine-stricken areas of the Soviet Union . . . in the hope of finding food there. By that time they were usually so weak that they mostly died on the street, so as a child I saw many deaths . . . whole families dying on the sidewalks."

SOURCE 6   By a writer, Nina Berberova, who was living in Petrograd in 1921

"A city completely dead . . . No electricity, no heat. It was a terrible city, because there was nothing . . . people just dying."

64

Opposition to Lenin's policies

Opposition to Communism grew as a result of the grim economic situation and the brutal way in which the Communists were running the country.

- A group called the **Workers' Opposition** was formed, demanding higher wages, better conditions, more food and workers' control of industry. One of their leaders was Alexandra Kollontai, the Bolshevik. She, like many other Bolsheviks and left-wingers, objected to the use of mass arrests by the Cheka to scare the people into submission. There were calls for 'Soviets without Communists'.

- In March 1921, sailors at the **Kronstadt naval base** (on an island just outside Petrograd) staged an uprising because 'life under the yoke of the Communist dictatorship has become more terrible than death'. The Red Kronstadters, as they were known, had been strong supporters of the Bolsheviks during the 1917 Revolution. By 1921 these were not the same men – most had gone off to fight in the Civil War – but the uprising was still a shock to the government. Trotsky had to use troops to crush them, and 20,000 men were killed and wounded in the attack. The sailors were executed in batches or sent off to labour camps.

1. What happened to industrial production between 1913 and 1921 (Source 2)?
2. Was this all the result of War Communism?
3. Where have you come across similar demands to those put forward by the Kronstadt sailors in Source 7?
4. Why do you think the Kronstadters fought so hard (Source 9)?

■ ACTIVITY

You are a policy adviser to Lenin. Persuade him that it is time to introduce a new economic policy. Give him your reasons, mentioning:

- economic consequences of the Civil War and War Communism
- the growth of opposition and the reasons for it.

SOURCE 7   Demands of the Kronstadt sailors

66 ■ *Because the present Soviets do not express the will of the workers and peasants, new elections should be held.*
- *Freedom of speech and press to be granted to workers and peasants.*
- *Also freedom of assembly and of trade unions and peasants' associations.*
- *All political prisoners belonging to Socialist parties . . . to be set free.* 99

SOURCE 8   Attack on Kronstadt across the ice, 17 March 1921

SOURCE 9   Tukhachevsky, leader of the attack on Kronstadt, made this report to Trotsky

66 *The sailors fought like wild beasts. I cannot understand where they found the might for such rage . . . An entire company fought for an hour to capture one house and when the house was captured it was found to contain two or three soldiers at a machine gun. They seemed half dead, but they snatched their revolvers and gasped, 'We didn't shoot enough of you bastards.'* 99

How successful was the NEP?

LENIN SAID that the Kronstadt rising was 'the flash that lit up reality'. He knew that he had to do something to improve the economic situation in Russia. If he did not, the Communists would not survive. In 1921, he introduced a New Economic Policy (NEP).

The main features of the NEP

- Grain requisitioning was stopped. No longer would grain be taken from the peasants by force. The peasants would have to give a fixed amount of grain to the government each year as a tax, but any surplus they produced could be sold on the open market.

- Traders could buy and sell goods (this had been illegal during War Communism).

- Smaller factories, particularly those producing consumer goods like shoes and clothes, were returned to their former owners. They were allowed to sell the goods they made and make a profit.

- Larger industries, e.g. coal, steel and transport, remained under state control. Some larger factories were allowed to sell their products.

Lenin said that the NEP would give the Soviet Union a 'breathing space' to get back on its feet. But many Communists were angry about what they saw as a return to capitalism. They did not like the idea that 'making a profit' was the main driving force for smaller industries. They disliked the fact that the bosses of factories or kulaks (rich peasants) could hire men to work for them. It was all too much like the old days.

Communists particularly disliked the new traders, who appeared in the cities. These 'Nepmen', as they were called, made high profits by buying food and goods cheaply and selling them more dearly. They were middlemen who, as the Communists saw it, made money out of the labour of others. But they made the goods appear in the shops in quantities that had not been seen for years. Nepmen also set up restaurants and made enormous amounts of money from dealing in property and gambling.

Lenin persuaded the Party to accept the NEP for the time being. The majority realised that these measures were needed to revive industry and get more food produced.

Electrification

One great step forward was the electrification of Russia. Lenin was enthusiastic about technological innovation and saw electric power as the key to modernising the Soviet Union. He envisaged a great network of power stations which would provide the power for modern large-scale industry. He wanted to put an electric light in every home to replace oil lamps and candles. Lenin believed electric power would change things so much that he said: 'Soviet power plus electrification equals Communism.'

1. Look at Source 1.
a) What do the horse and sledge represent?
b) Who is on the sledge?
c) Why should Kamenev want to stop the sledge?
2. Why do you think Lenin placed such importance on electricity as a means of changing life in Soviet Russia? Think about its uses today.

SOURCE 1 A 1924 cartoon entitled 'Honorary militiaman, L.B. Kamenev'. Kamenev was a leading Communist. The horse has NEP written on its collar

SOURCE 2 A poster celebrating the electrification of Russia

SOURCE 3 Fitting the first electric bulb in a Russian village, 1928

Foreign trade

NEP encouraged foreign countries, which had refused to trade with Soviet Russia before 1921, to resume trade links. Western countries hoped that the move back to private trade and profit – capitalism – meant the failure of Communist ideas. An Anglo-Soviet trade agreement in 1921 marked the beginning of increased trade with the West which gave a great boost to the Soviet economy. There were large-scale exchanges of Western industrial goods for Russian oil and similar products.

Success and failure

The NEP lasted until 1928 and Russia generally became more prosperous. Some of this can be put down to the period of stability which followed seven years of war and civil war from 1914 to 1921. But the NEP undoubtedly played a big role in improving the general economic situation.

However, NEP was far from a total success story. The peasants found prices for manufactured goods high and were unwilling, after 1925, to sell their grain for money because they could not buy much with it. While some peasants became quite rich buying up land and animals, many remained poor and continued to use backward methods of farming. Industrial workers were better off but levels of unemployment remained a serious problem for the whole time of the NEP, particularly among young people, and there was a high crime rate associated with this. Many people were angry about the profiteering of the Nepmen and the growth of a class of rich businessmen. After 1925 steps were taken to curb their profits and luxurious lifestyle.

Up to 1925, much of the progress under NEP had been from very low levels of production and involved repairing and restoring old machinery, factories and transport. But by 1926 the economy had reached pre-1914 levels and massive new investment was needed to turn the Soviet Union into a modern industrialised country. Where was this going to come from? Also, by the end of the 1920s, food supplies were a problem again, and many Communists wanted to see the introduction of more Socialist methods of running the economy.

SOURCE 4 From *I Write As I Please*, 1935, by Walter Duranty. Duranty was an American journalist who was in Russia during the NEP

"Moscow had changed during my three weeks' absence. Everywhere run-down and half-ruined buildings were being refurbished and restored. Shops, cafes and restaurants were being opened in all directions . . . The city was full of peasants selling fruit, vegetables and other produce . . .

To the Communists NEP was doubtless repugnant, but to the mass of the workers it brought jobs that would be paid in money instead of valueless paper or mouldy rations, and the certainty that with money they could buy the food and necessities of life . . .

To the traders, NEP meant opportunity and the dawn of better days. Until August 9th (1921) it was technically a crime to possess goods of value . . . and a crime to buy and sell anything. The NEP decree changed all that . . .

At the top of my street, I saw a man selling flour, sugar and rice on a little table . . . At the end of a week he was selling fresh eggs and vegetables . . . By mid-November he had rented a tiny store . . . By the following May he had four salesmen in a fair-sized store, to which peasants brought fresh produce each morning. After a year's trading . . . he made $20,000 to $30,000 clear profit, but the point is that his enterprise stimulated scores of peasants to fatten chickens or little pigs or plant vegetables. The same thing was being done all over Russia and the effects were amazing. In a single year the supply of food and goods jumped from starvation point to something nearly adequate, and prices fell accordingly. "

SOURCE 5 From a 1923 report by Walter Duranty

"Living conditions in Russia have enormously improved in the past two years.

The condition of Moscow may be reckoned as 25 per cent ahead of the rest of Russia, but similar, if slower, improvement is visible everywhere. The essential fact is that everyone is so infinitely better off than during the 'black years' of 1920 and 1921 that present conditions seem paradise by comparison.

The industrial workers are relatively better off although hit by high prices and short time in many industries . . . at least they get paid regularly now . . .

The industrial workers of Moscow grumble about the overcrowding and the luxury displayed by the 'Nepmen', the newly rich traders and speculators . . . It is estimated that upward of 250,000 private traders have migrated to Moscow since the NEP began, two years ago. They crowd the restaurants where it costs $25 a head for dinner with French wine . . . and lose a thousand or so an evening at baccarat [cards] without turning a hair. "

1. What do the figures in Source 6 show about:
a) changes in the production of grain under NEP?
b) changes in industrial output?
2. a) Do these figures show that NEP was a complete success?
b) Why do you have to be careful about accepting these figures?

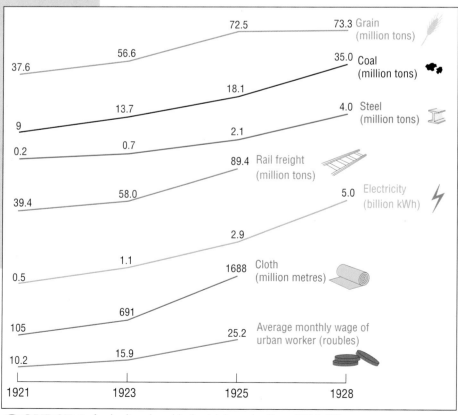

SOURCE 6 Agricultural and industrial production, 1921–28

SOURCE 7 General Grigovenko of the Soviet army recalling the time

"Never did I live as well as I did in the NEP years, not even when I became a general."

SOURCE 8 Anna Strong, a Communist

"In my few short trips into Moscow during the winter of 1921–22, I had been disturbed by the growing private trade. To me each seems a step of defeat . . . There's a horrible new rich set growing."

3. a) How do Sources 2, 4, 5 and 7 support the view that the NEP was successful?
b) How does the writer of Source 4 account for this?
4. How do Sources 1 and 8 explain why many Communists did not like NEP?

■ ACTIVITY

1. Use all the information to make a balance sheet for the NEP. On one side put the positive aspects of NEP, on the other put the negative aspects.
2. How do you think that each of the following would respond to the question 'Do you think that the NEP was good for Russia?'?

■ a peasant
■ a member of the Communist Party
■ a private trader
■ an industrial worker.

chapter 6

DID THE COMMUNIST REVOLUTION CHANGE RUSSIA IN THE 1920s?

How did the Communists try to change Russia?

> **SOURCE 1** Ella Shister talking about the 1920s in an interview for *The People's Century*, a BBC programme shown in the 1990s
>
> *"What I liked was the promise of a happy classless society in the future in which everybody would enjoy the good created by society . . . When Lenin said that Communism is Soviet power plus electrification, I decided that I should become an electrical engineer . . . I wanted to build an electrical power station – that was my mission and I achieved it. The Revolution gave me the right to feel equal to any man, the right to study what I wanted to study."*

AS WE HAVE seen, life was very hard under War Communism. It took a long time for the country to recover from the depths of 1921. But how was life different in the 1920s from life before the Revolution? How had the Revolution changed things?

Equality, the family and the role of women

Some of the Bolsheviks' first actions (see page 50) were to abolish ranks and titles and to declare equality for women. They hoped to create a new era of freedom in personal and sexual relations. Alexandra Kollontai said that sex should be as natural as drinking a glass of water, and argued for free love. She headed a campaign to free women from the drudgery of family life by setting up creches and kindergartens. Marriage and divorce were made easy – simply a matter of both parties agreeing and filling in a register. Abortion was to be available on demand.

Despite this, the idea of the family proved very resistant to change, with few workers and peasants wanting to see it break down. Many did not agree with the new ideas on sex and marriage. Women did, however, gain more equality in the workplace.

Religion

Religion, which Communists saw as a trick to make people accept terrible conditions on earth in the hope of a better afterlife, came under attack. It was forbidden to teach religion to people under fifteen, and some churches were taken over and priests exiled.

Education

The Communists put a lot of effort into education, building schools and making sure that children got adequate food. In an attempt to capture the minds of the young, the Communist Party set up the Komsomol, or Young Communist League, to encourage the growth of Communist ideas. A massive literacy programme was begun, with thousands of young activists sent out to teach workers and peasants to read.

SOURCE 2 A poster with the slogan 'You are now a free woman – help to build Socialism!'

SOURCE 3 A church being used as a grain store in the late 1920s

Ideas

S OURCE 4   The agitprop train

S OURCE 5   The agitprop boat

S OURCE 6   A poster showing a man and woman working together. The slogan says, 'We destroyed the enemy with weapons, we'll earn our bread with labour – Comrades, roll up your sleeves for work!'

S OURCE 7   A poster showing a worker chained and a capitalist eating food

The Communists realised early on that they were a small group controlling a country which was still inhabited by peasants. They felt that they needed to explain the ideas of Communism to the people. They sent out 'agitprop' (agitation and propaganda) trains, boats and even trams to put across the messages of the Revolution and encourage Russians to see what they were working for in the future. They used posters, pamphlets and theatre groups, who acted out scenes about the aims of the new Socialist state. Many Russians saw their first films on the agitprop train. This propaganda machine was fed by the avant-garde art of the period.

S OURCE 8   An abstract painting from around 1919

S OURCE 9   Fabric with paintings of trains on it

S OURCE 10   A poster for the Blue Blouse theatre group

The arts

Experimentation in the arts was encouraged in film, painting, posters, sculpture, the theatre and radio. It was a time of great creativity. Young artists, poets and playwrights were excited by the ideas of the Revolution – a new society based on equal rights for the people. They abandoned the old forms of Tsarist art and looked to the future. They called themselves Futurists.

They believed in art for the people – art with a practical purpose. This was to be seen in the design of buildings, streets, fabrics, clothes, furniture and all areas of life. Architects constructed new types of housing and theatres.

The arts were affected by the new spirit of equality. Artists worked in teams. Orchestras did away with conductors, taking votes on how they wanted the music arranged.

Communist films, such as those made by Sergei Eisenstein – *October* and *Battleship Potemkin* – were amongst the most innovative made in the world at the time. Novelists such as Boris Pasternak and poets such as Osip Mandelstam flourished.

S OURCE 11   Designs for sportswear in the magazine *LEF*
S ('Left Front of the Arts'), 1923

SOURCE 12   Designs by Rodchenko for *Dobrolyet*

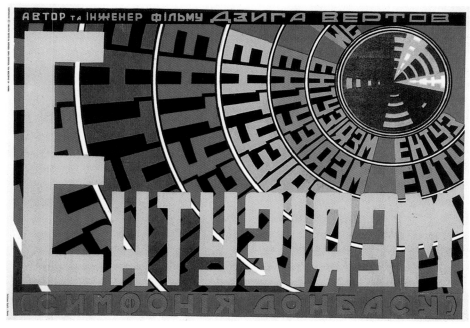

SOURCE 13   A poster for the film *Enthusiasm*

1. List three ways in which life for women changed in this period.
2. Why do you think the people resisted some of these changes?
3. What attitudes to women are shown in Sources 1, 2 and 6?
4. What methods did the Communists use to explain the ideas of the Revolution to the people?
5. What are the messages of Sources 6 and 7?
6. What part did Soviet art play in this idea of a new society?
7. Look at Sources 8–13.
a) How do they suggest a 'modern' view of art?
b) Choose three and explain why you would not have seen them in Tsarist Russia.
c) How do you think this 'art for the people' was different from art before the Revolution?

■ ACTIVITY

You are a foreign journalist visiting Russia, who has heard about exciting new changes since the Revolution. Write an article for your newspaper back home. Include in it:

■ changes in attitudes to the role of women in society
■ the role of the family and the Church
■ education and ways of explaining the new Communist ideas
■ changes in the arts.

Comment on how far these changes are going and whether everybody agrees with them.

Select two illustrations from pages 70–73 which best sum up these changes to go with your article.

A Russian village in the 1920s

IN 1926, Maurice Hindus, who had lived most of his life in America, went back to the village where he was born. He never names the village. The following extracts show what he found.

SOURCE 1   A description of the old village

There was the same long, narrow winding street, as in the old days, still unpaved, and now after the heavy rain of the previous day and night, turned into a river of black slush . . . No sidewalks; not a patch of lawn, not a flower bush; the little heaps of manure lying as of old at every house right by the open wall.

The same muddy street, the same dwarfed houses with the puny windows and thatch roofs, the same foul smells, the same scene of poverty and helplessness.

Fields were as in former times cut into narrow strips, narrower than in my boyhood days . . . too small to grow enough bread even for a mere man and wife. Yet there were families in the village that had to live off such puny holdings.

SOURCE 2   At the village mill, Hindus talked to some villagers

That these peasants mistrusted the Soviet government was clear enough. After all it was a government, something that exacted obligations which they were loath to fulfil, just as the old government did . . .

'What I'd like to know is what these Soviets do with all their money. Just think of the amounts they gather as fines alone, and then taxes . . .'

'Aye,' said Fyodor, 'if I had half of what they took in today, I could buy boots for everyone in my family.'

Demyan: 'They are spending it on themselves. That's why they all sport around in new boots, all of them, from the chairman of the Soviet to the lowest clerk.'

'And why shouldn't they?' queried another man (Zakhar). 'They are our rulers, aren't they? Well, rulers always do have everything. Think of the Tsar and the landlords and the generals in the old days. They did not lack anything, did they? Indeed not, for they were our rulers.'

SOURCE 3 He talked to young people in the village

66*And what, I asked, of the morality of the young people? Had there been any changes since the Revolution? None, they replied. Girls were as strict as ever their mothers and grandmothers had been.*

Of course a fellow could flirt with a girl, put his arm around her, hold her hand, kiss her – but only on the cheek or neck, never on the lips, unless she was his fiancée. Otherwise – well – our girls were quite strong, a blow of their fists might even draw blood . . .

Lapses in conduct were as rare as in the old times . . . it was the worst thing for a girl to submit to a man. Her betrayer is likely to abandon her; and no other man, excepting perhaps one old enough to be her grandfather, would have her as a wife. The girls knew that and took care of themselves.

And what, I further inquired, of the Young Communists? . . . They laughed uproariously. Ekh, the Young Communists! There were only two in our village, and there were not many more in any of the villages around, and some should retire to a monastery . . . Some of them were against kissing and dancing, said it was all the invention of the capitalists to corrupt the peasant and prole- tarian . . . and besides it was too much responsibility to be a Young Communist, too many meetings to attend, too stern a discipline to submit to; and they were fearfully strict.

And then I shifted the conversation to religion . . . The girls, they informed me, were quite loyal to the Church, just like their mothers. Of course, they no longer attended services as regularly as they had in former times . . . Still, when they married they insisted on a church wedding, but the problem of church weddings was beginning to cause no little trouble in the villages. No real revolutionary, especially if he was a member of the Communist Party, would have a priest marry him. 99

SOURCE 4 What supporters of the Revolution said

66*'And there is no more standing to attention until your feet sink under you and your bones crack, and there is no more "your highness" or "your excellency". It is all tovarish [comrade] now . . .'*

'When the muzhik [peasant] boy goes to the army, nobody weeps. He goes away for only a short time, and during his service his family get a reduction in the amount of their taxes, and when he comes back he can read and write. He knows who Marx was and what he taught. He understands the class struggle. He believes in the Revolution.'

'Yes,' chimed in another youth, 'and a muzhik is now given preference in the university, and he pays nothing for his studies there, and if he is poor he is given board and room free.'

'. . . and a muzhik, tovarishtsh, can climb as high in rank as his ability will permit. That's something isn't it?' 99

■ TASK

1. Draw a chart like the one below to show how the Revolution had changed lives in the village.

What had changed	What had stayed the same

2. Do you think the changes were for the better or the worse?
3. Can the example of one village help us understand how the Revolution was affecting villages throughout the USSR?

Was Lenin a great leader?

The death of Lenin

LENIN DIED in January 1924, aged 53. When doctors examined his brain, they found that it had shrunk to almost half its normal size. Lenin, who had suffered several strokes since 1922, had been overwhelmed by the enormously long hours he had worked after the Revolution.

Thousands lined the streets as his coffin was carried to Red Square in Moscow, and came to see him lying in state. After his death he was embalmed, and a mausoleum was built to house his body. Petrograd was renamed Leningrad, and huge amounts of Lenin memorabilia, such as ashtrays in the shape of the mausoleum, began to appear. He became the centre of a semi-religious Lenin cult.

 **S**OURCE 1   The queue to see Lenin's body

Different interpretations

Historians have given very different interpretations of Lenin's role in Russia between 1917 and 1924. Often, these are connected with the political views of the historians. Soviet and Marxist historians have praised Lenin's achievements as the founder of the Soviet state; for them, he could do no wrong. Historians in the West have mixed views. Some have seen him as a tyrant who seized power for his own ends and inflicted terrible suffering on the Russian people. Others believe he was an able leader, with basically good intentions and qualities, who nevertheless created a dictatorship based on terror.

Here are some of the points historians have made for and against him.

For
- He was a modest man who did not have any personal ambition.
- He was a very good speaker who could sway audiences.
- He had excellent leadership qualities.
- Without him there would not have been a revolution in November 1917. He persuaded the other Bolsheviks to seize power.
- He had superb organising skills. He kept Russia going.
- It was largely due to Lenin that the Bolsheviks were able to stay in power after 1917. He had good political judgement and was able to adapt to changing circumstances.
- He had to use the Cheka and terror because of the Civil War and chaos between 1917 and 1924. He was beginning to allow more freedom after 1921.

Against
- He seized power with a small group of people without the support of most of the population. This led to a dictatorship.
- He would not share power with other Socialists, especially the Socialist Revolutionaries, who had won the elections to the Constituent Assembly. This made the Civil War much worse than it might have been.
- He used ruthless methods and terror to stay in power.
- He was prepared to see millions of Russians suffer for his ideals.
- He stopped other people expressing their opinions.
- He made the Communist Party an organisation for carrying out orders. Members were not allowed to disagree with the leaders.

■ TASK

1. Draw a table like the one below. Choose four statements for Lenin and four against him. Put these in the left-hand column. Then find evidence for each statement and put this in the right-hand column. Two statements have been put in for you. You can find the evidence in the work you have done on Lenin in this book.

FOR

Statement	Evidence
He was a modest man who did not have any personal ambition.	Never became rich. While leader, lived a simple life, e.g. slept on an iron bed in a carpetless room. Did not like praise.

AGAINST

Statement	Evidence
He stopped other people expressing their opinions.	Shut down other political parties and newspapers. People who put opposing views were arrested.

2. In what ways do Sources 2, 3 and 5 agree?
3. Why might Gorky's opinions in Source 2 be more trustworthy than some others?
4. a) What is Christopher Hill's view of Lenin?
   b) How does he explain away the harsh judgements of Lenin's government?

SOURCE 2   By Maxim Gorky, writer and early supporter of Bolsheviks, and Lenin's friend

"Lenin is a gifted man who has all the qualities of a leader, including these essential ones: lack of morality and a merciless, lordly harshness towards the lives of the masses . . . As long as I can, I will repeat to the Russian proletariat, 'You are being led to destruction, you are being used as material in an inhuman experiment; to your leaders, you are not human.'"

SOURCE 3   From *Lenin and the Bolsheviks* by Adam Ulam

"It must be an indelible stain on Lenin's record that for all his humane instincts he allowed this cult . . . of terror to develop . . . He allowed mass terror not only to be practised, but to become legitimate and respectable."

SOURCE 4   From Christopher Hill, *Lenin and the Russian Revolution*, 1947. The author, a Marxist historian, supported the aims of the Russian Revolution

"First and foremost Lenin symbolises the Russian Revolution as a movement of the poor and oppressed . . . against the great and the powerful . . . Lenin possessed a second quality – humaneness. Thirdly, Lenin stands for . . . purposefulness, realism, common sense, will-power . . .

We must judge the successes and failures . . . as part of an experiment which had unexpectedly to be made in conditions of quite exceptional difficulty, with desperately inadequate resources, material and human . . ."

SOURCE 5   From *Lenin: an Autobiography* by David Shub, 1969

"Lenin might well have said: 'I created the Bolshevik Party. I was the brain of the November Revolution. Several times, when our power seemed about to crumble, I saved it . . .' Lenin could rightfully have said this, but never did, for no dictator in history was less vain. He was repelled by all attempts to set him on a pedestal . . .

He remained true to a single idea and a single aim . . . the cause of the proletarian revolution . . . Russia was his laboratory for testing Communism on a grand scale; the immediate welfare of the Russian people was secondary."

■ ACTIVITY

Write an obituary for Lenin. Write this from one of the positions listed below:

■ a supporter of Lenin's achievements in Russia
■ someone who believes Lenin seized power on behalf of a small group of people and set up a tyrannical regime based on terror.

For your obituary, use:

■ the evidence you have collected for the task on page 77
■ the sources on page 77
■ any other information you can find.

Ask your teacher for the support sheet.

SOURCE 6   Lenin's body lying in state

STALIN'S USSR: WAS STALIN A DISASTER FOR THE USSR?

chapter 7

HOW DID STALIN BECOME LEADER OF THE USSR?

Where did Stalin come from?

UNLIKE OTHER LEADERS of the Communist Party, Stalin did not have a middle-class background. He was born in eastern Georgia in 1879; his father was a cobbler and his mother a peasant. They were poor, and Joseph Djugashvili (Stalin's real name) had a hard upbringing. He did well at school and gained a scholarship to a seminary (a college for training priests) in Tbilisi. But at the seminary, the young Joseph found Marxism rather than God. He became involved in the underground world of the revolutionaries, writing pamphlets and attending secret meetings. He greatly admired the writings of Lenin.

SOURCE 1   A photograph of Stalin as a revolutionary

Joseph became an active revolutionary, organising strikes and possibly carrying out bank robberies to raise funds for the Bolsheviks. Between 1902 and 1913 he was arrested and exiled to Siberia eight times (escaping on seven occasions). He became harder as the years passed, especially after the death of his first wife in 1909. In the prison camps, he gained the name of Stalin, which means 'man of steel'. One story says that he was given this name because he used to bend bars of steel over his back.

When the Revolution of March 1917 broke out, Stalin hurried back to Petrograd, where he was made editor of *Pravda* ('Truth'), the Party newspaper. There is no evidence of Stalin taking charge of any of the events during the Revolution; it seems that his skill lay in working within the party organisation, a skill he was to use to his advantage later on. After the November Revolution, he was made Commissar for Nationalities.

In 1922 he was appointed the Party's first General Secretary, in charge of general organisation. This job was seen as dull and routine by the other Bolsheviks.

1. The painting in Source 2 was made after Stalin had become leader of the Soviet Union.
a) What do you think was the reason for painting this picture?
b) Do you think it tells us anything about Stalin's childhood?
c) What is this picture good evidence of?

SOURCE 2   A painting of Stalin as a child, teaching a group of other children. Stalin is sitting in the centre

Stalin or Trotsky?

AFTER LENIN'S DEATH, the main contenders to be the new leader of the Communist Party were Stalin and Trotsky.

Trotsky

When Lenin died, Trotsky seemed the most likely candidate to become the new leader. He had planned the November Revolution. His organisation of the Red Army had led to victory in the Civil War. He was a well-known figure, popular with the Red Army and younger Party members.

Trotsky was the only leading Communist who could rival Lenin as a speaker and writer about revolutionary ideas. But he did not inspire affection in the way Lenin did. He was arrogant and did not have a lot of time for those he considered stupid. He refused to get involved in the dirty business of political in-fighting, making alliances and getting people on his side.

Trotsky believed in helping Communists in other countries to stage revolutions, by giving them money and sending agents. He also wanted to push forward the revolution inside the USSR: he wanted to end the NEP and bring in more socialist ways of running the economy. He called his policies **'Permanent Revolution'**.

Many older Party members distrusted Trotsky. They were worried that he might become a dictator, especially as he could count on the Red Army to support him. They doubted his loyalty to the Party as he had not joined the Bolshevik Party until 1917. They also thought his extreme views would split the Party at a time when unity was needed.

For three years from the end of 1923, Trotsky suffered attacks of fever. The illness sapped his strength and left him less able to deal with the continuous attacks on him mounted by his enemies.

Stalin

Stalin had a very powerful position as General Secretary of the Communist Party. He could appoint people to posts and had control of the membership of the Party. Between 1922 and 1924, he put more and more of his own supporters into important Party positions. He also expelled from the Party the younger, wilder and more radical elements likely to support Trotsky. Other Bolsheviks allowed him to do this because they were worried about Trotsky taking control as a dictator.

Stalin was the opposite of Trotsky. He was not an intellectual or an inspiring speaker. He was regarded as dull, mediocre and humourless by other leading Communists. However, he was politically cunning, playing off different groups in the Communist Party against each other. He was happy to stay in the background, building up his support.

Stalin believed that the Russians could build a Communist state in the USSR without the help of people from outside. He called his policy **'Socialism in One Country'**.

Stalin had been a loyal member of the Party for over twenty years. He was a safe, middle-of-the-road Communist, who did not hold extreme views that would be likely to split the Party.

A warning from Lenin

Stalin had a serious problem to overcome if he wanted to become leader – Lenin's testament. Lenin had become very concerned about Stalin and his growing power. He had found out that, in 1921, Stalin had brutally put down the Georgians. Stalin had also insulted Lenin's wife. Lenin detected a dangerous aspect in Stalin's personality and in his last testament warned against him (see Source 1).

SOURCE 1

❝ Comrade Stalin, having become General Secretary, has great power concentrated in his hands, and I am not sure that he always knows how to use that power with sufficient caution.

Later he added:

Stalin is too rude, and this fault . . . becomes unacceptable in the office of General Secretary. Therefore, I propose to the comrades that a way be found to remove Stalin from that post and replace him with someone else who differs from Stalin in all respects, someone more patient, more loyal, more polite, more considerate. ❞

The struggle for power

The struggle for the leadership of the Communist Party was a battle of ideas as well as people. The Communist Party had a left wing and a right wing. Stalin was in the middle of the Party.

Left wing of the Party

Zinoviev   Kamenev

■ TASK

1. Draw two charts, one for Trotsky and one for Stalin. List the factors working for and against each person in the leadership struggle. Use the information above to start the chart and add to it as you work through this section. The first chart has been started for you below.

Trotsky

Factors for	Factors against
■ Organised the November Revolution	■ Not trusted by other Communists

2. Imagine you are a member of the Communist Party in the USSR in 1924. There have been seven years of hardship since 1917. Would you find Trotsky's 'Permanent Revolution' or Stalin's 'Socialism in One Country' more appealing?
3. What do you think would have happened to Stalin's chances of becoming leader if the testament had been made public?
4. Add this to your Stalin chart.

Zinoviev and Kamenev were old Bolsheviks. They shared the same ideas as Trotsky, but disliked him and were worried that he would become a dictator. The left wing of the Party wanted to end the NEP, quicken the pace of industrialisation using 'shock brigades' of workers, and force the peasants to produce the food they needed.

Right wing of the Party

Bukharin had one of the best brains in the Party. He was convinced that the NEP was the way forward: he thought that if the peasants became richer they would buy more goods, which would help industry grow, and everybody would become more prosperous. The right wing wanted to move slowly towards Socialism.

Bukharin

1 Stalin gained the first advantage over Trotsky at Lenin's funeral. Trotsky was ill and Stalin tricked him into not coming. People thought Trotsky could not be bothered to turn up. Stalin made a big speech praising Lenin and said he was Lenin's disciple.

2 The leading Communists decided not to make Lenin's testament public as it contained criticisms of them as well as of Stalin. Stalin heaved a big sigh of relief.

3 In 1924, at the first Party Congress after Lenin's death, Zinoviev and Kamenev joined forces with Stalin to defeat Trotsky. Stalin, as Party Secretary, made sure that his supporters packed the Congress. Trotsky lost all the votes and soon after lost his job as Commissar for the War. He no longer controlled the Red Army.

4 In 1926, Stalin turned on Zinoviev and Kamenev. He joined forces with Bukharin and the right wing of the Party, putting forward his ideas on Socialism in One Country. Once again, Stalin's supporters packed the Congress and he easily won the votes on important issues. Zinoviev and Kamenev lost their jobs in the Politburo.

5 In 1927, Trotsky, Zinoviev and Kamenev were expelled from the Party.

6 Finally, Stalin turned on Bukharin and right-wing MPs. He attacked the NEP, which they supported, and had them removed from their posts. In 1929, Stalin celebrated his 50th birthday as the undisputed leader of the USSR.

■ TASK

1. Identify the factors which worked for Stalin and against Trotsky and add them to your chart.

2. Draw a flow diagram to show how Stalin became leader after Lenin's funeral. ➤

Why did Stalin win?

■ SOURCE INVESTIGATION

SOURCE 1   John Reed, an American journalist who was in Russia during the Revolution, said of Stalin

❝*He's not an intellectual like the other people you will meet . . . but he knows what he wants. He's got willpower, and he's going to be top of the pile some day.*❞

SOURCE 2   From an interview with Michael Voslensky, a high-ranking Soviet official

❝*The key to Stalin's rise to the top was that he succeeded in concentrating all appointments to key positions in the country in his own hands.*❞

SOURCE 3   From an interview with Nadezhda Ioffe, daughter of an old Bolshevik

❝*Nobody felt he represented any danger. For example, Zinoviev and Kamenev would not have liked to see Bukharin having the role of General Secretary, and Bukharin would not have liked to see Zinoviev having that post, and all of them agreed that they were afraid of Trotsky . . . but nobody seemed particularly opposed to the idea of Stalin having the post and that's why it happened in the end – he got such a large amount of power in his hands.*❞

SOURCE 4   Iosfi Itskov, a Party member in 1924, said of Stalin

❝*He tried to stay in the shadows . . . He was a man whose aim was very clear, but you could never tell how he was going to accomplish it. He accomplished it in the most cunning way. And he allowed nothing to get in his way.*❞

SOURCE 5   From *The Prophet Unarmed, Trotsky 1921–29*, by I. Deutscher

❝*Trotsky did not attack Stalin because he felt secure. No contemporary saw in the Stalin of 1923 the menacing and towering figure he was to become. It seemed to Trotsky almost a bad joke that Stalin, the wilful and sly but shabby and inarticulate man in the background, should be his rival.*❞

SOURCE 6   From *The Prophet Unarmed, Trotsky 1921–29*, by I. Deutscher

❝*While on a train travelling south to recuperate from his illness, Trotsky said that he received a telegram from Stalin telling him of Lenin's death and that . . . 'the funeral would be held on the 26th; since he would be unable to return in time, he should continue travelling south'. The telegram lied: the funeral was to be held a day later, on the 27th, giving Trotsky ample time to attend . . . Trotsky, it was widely felt, had not bothered to turn up. It was a serious political error and dealt a fatal blow to Trotsky's prestige.*❞

1. Each source (1–6) gives a reason why Stalin won the power struggle. Identify each reason and add it to your Stalin chart.
2. In what ways was Trotsky responsible for his own downfall? Add these to your Trotsky chart.

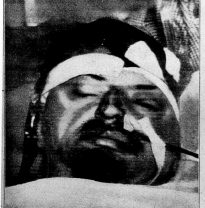

↑ **Trotsky Death Weapon**
Mexican policemen show short-handled pickaxe with which Frank Jackson fatally wounded the exiled Leon Trotsky, military genius of the Russian Revolution. Jackson, beaten by police, is recovering in hospital where Trotsky died. —*Story p. 2.*

← **Dying, He Blamed Stalin**
In pain-wracked hours of his battle for life in Mexico City hospital Trotsky knew death was

SOURCE 7   Trotsky is reported as dead in the *Daily News*, an American newspaper

■ ACTIVITY

1. Look through your charts on Stalin and Trotsky.
a) From your list of 'factors for' Stalin, choose two which you think were the most important.
b) From your list of 'factors against' Trotsky, choose the two you think were most important.
2. Use your charts to write an account of how Stalin became the supreme leader of the USSR.

You could divide this into three sections:

A Explain the factors working for Stalin. Start with the ones you think were most important.
B Explain the factors working against Trotsky.
C Explain how Stalin used circumstances to his advantage. For example:
   ■ how he used Lenin's funeral
   ■ how he allied himself to different groups in the Party to get rid of his opponents.

What happened to Trotsky?

In 1928 Trotsky found himself being bundled onto a train in his pyjamas and sent off to central Asia. Stalin still regarded him as a threat and had him expelled from the USSR altogether in 1929.

No country could be found to offer Trotsky asylum, but eventually he was allowed to settle in Turkey. He immediately set about writing his history of the Revolution and started to create an international Communist movement. For the next ten years, he wrote articles attacking Stalin and was a constant thorn in his side.

Trotsky remained worried about his first wife and children, who were still in the USSR – rightly, in fact, as his son Sergei died in a concentration camp. Trotsky's elder son, Leon, died in Paris in 1937, probably killed by the Russian secret police.

After 1933, Trotsky moved to France and then to Oslo in Norway. But Trotsky's political activities made him unwelcome, and in 1937 he went to Mexico. Trotsky was always under threat, and several of his close associates were murdered. The Soviet secret police had spies inside his household, and attempts were made on his life.

On 20 August 1940, Trotsky's luck ran out. A hired hit man, Ramon Mercador, gained access to Trotsky in his study. Mercador had asked Trotsky to comment on an article he had written. He later testified:

I put my raincoat on a piece of furniture. I took out the ice-pick [hidden in my coat] and, closing my eyes, brought it down on his head with all my strength . . . he uttered a terrible piercing cry – I shall hear that cry all my life.

Trotsky was taken to hospital but died the next day. The autopsy showed a brain of 'extraordinary dimension'.

chapter 8

WERE STALIN'S ECONOMIC POLICIES A SUCCESS OR A FAILURE?

Why did the Soviet Union need to change?

IN 1928, the USSR was still a poor, backward country, producing fewer industrial goods than many smaller countries. Stalin aimed to transform it into a modern, powerful industrial nation.

There were three main reasons for developing industry quickly:

- to provide the machinery, especially tractors, needed to mechanise farming and produce more food
- to catch up with the Western world and make Russia less dependent on the West for industrial goods
- to have a strong industry capable of producing armaments so that Russia could defend itself from attack.

But to develop industry, it was also necessary to develop agriculture. Agriculture in the USSR was still not very sophisticated, and Stalin needed to produce more food, especially grain, to feed the growing number of workers. He also needed to export grain to foreign countries in order to earn foreign currency to buy essential industrial machinery and goods. Stalin chose to change agriculture by collectivisation (see pages 95–101).

1. Why was it so important to the Communists to industrialise the USSR?
2. Why was agriculture so closely linked to industrial development?
3. Why, according to Stalin in Source 2, was it important to make the changes quickly?
4. a) What image of Stalin is presented in Source 1?
   b) Why would Stalin want the Russian people to see this poster?

SOURCE 1   A propaganda poster showing Stalin marching alongside miners, made during the first Five-Year Plan

SOURCE 2   From Stalin's Collected Works, 1931

We must . . . create in our country an industry which would be capable of re-equipping and organising not only the whole of our industry but also our transport and our agriculture . . . The history of Russia shows . . . that because of her backwardness she was constantly being defeated . . . We are 50 or 100 years behind the advanced countries. We must make good this lag in ten years. Either we do it or we will go under.

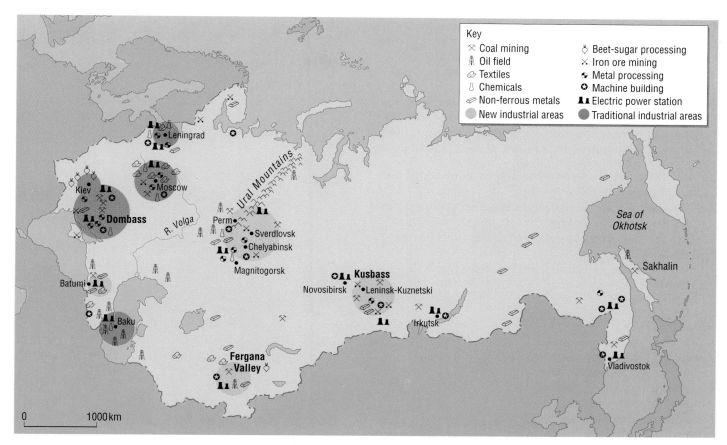

Key
✕ Coal mining
⛏ Oil field
☁ Textiles
◊ Chemicals
⬖ Non-ferrous metals
◯ New industrial areas
◔ Beet-sugar processing
✕ Iron ore mining
✦ Metal processing
✪ Machine building
⚡ Electric power station
⬤ Traditional industrial areas

SOURCE 1   A map showing the new industrial centres

The planned economy

Stalin and the Communist Party believed that the way to develop industry and run the economy was through state planning. The state would determine not only what should be produced, but also how, when and where it would be produced. It also determined prices and wages. To organise this sort of planning, the idea of Five-Year Plans was adopted. The detailed planning of the economy was carried out by Gosplan, the state planning agency.

Five-Year Plans	
First:	1928–32
Second:	1933–37
Third:	1938–41 (interrupted by the Second World War)

1. Why did Stalin build the new industrial centres so far to the east, a long way from Moscow and St Petersburg?
2. How is a free-market economy different from a planned economy?

How did the Five-Year Plans work?

The plans set production targets, which industries had to reach. For example, the coal industry was set the target of producing 75 million tons of coal by 1932. To achieve this, coal-producing areas and local managers were given their own specific targets. Source 2 shows the production targets set by each plan.

■ The first Five-Year Plan emphasised heavy industries – coal, oil, iron and steel, electricity – to lay the foundations for future industrial growth. The targets set were unbelievably high and unrealistic, but remarkable results were achieved. Coal and iron both doubled their output; electric power production almost trebled; 1,500 new industrial plants were built. The building of over 100 new towns, some carved out of nothing, was started.

- The second Five-Year Plan gave heavy industry top priority, but communications, especially railways, became important to link cities and industrial centres. New industries, such as chemicals and metallurgy, grew enormously.
- The third Five-Year Plan ran for only three years, up to 1941, when Russia entered the Second World War. As war approached, more resources were put into developing armaments – tanks, planes and weapons.

1. From the figures in Source 2, how successful do the plans seem to have been?
2. Why might you be worried about accepting figures produced by the Soviet government?
3. Why do you think the idea of using targets was effective?
4. Stalin always declared the Five-Year Plans completed a year ahead of schedule. Can you explain why?

SOURCE 2   Production figures for 1927 (before the first Five-Year Plan), and for the first two Five-Year Plans, in millions of tons. Production targets are shown in brackets

	1927	1932	1937
Coal	35	64 (75)	128 (152)
Oil	12	21 (22)	29 (47)
Iron ore	5	12 (19)	not known
Pig iron	3	6 (10)	15 (16)
Steel	4	6 (10)	18 (17)

Specialists

Stalin brought in specialist advisers from other countries to help develop industry. There were a lot of British and American engineers. The Dnieper dam project was carried out under the supervision of an American, as was the building of the Soviet asbestos industry. The Ford motor company helped the Soviet car industry to build 140,000 cars in 1932.

Single managers

Stalin reintroduced single managers to run state enterprises and factories. The idea of workers' control was left far behind. Stalin thought he would get better results from individual managers who were directly responsible for the targets they had to fulfil. Trade unions were told not to interfere. Managers who did well were richly rewarded, many receiving large houses and motor cars.

Spectacular achievements

A feature of all the plans in the 1930s were spectacular building projects, held up as showpieces of Soviet achievement. These included the dam on the River Dnieper in eastern Russia, the Moscow–Volga canal and the Moscow Metro – an underground train system with stunning stations built on a grand scale.

S OURCE 3   The Dnieprostroi Dam, built in the 1930s

If things go wrong, blame the workers

Despite these apparent successes, the central planning was not very efficient. In some industries there was over-production, in others under-production, so that factories were kept idle for weeks, waiting for essential parts. Yet the drive was always to fulfil the targets at any cost. Some of the goods produced were almost unusable because they had been turned out so quickly by untrained workers. Mistakes were made: machines were unwittingly wrecked by unskilled workers, many of them ex-peasants who had been used to only the most primitive levels of technology.

But these mistakes could not be admitted – the system could not be at fault. So 'wreckers' or 'saboteurs' were found and blamed. As early as 1928, when the coal mines in the Donbass region fell behind target, 53 engineers were accused of conspiracy to wreck the Soviet coal-mining industry. This led to the famous Shakhty trial. Other SHOW TRIALS were to follow.

The hysteria and fear created by the trials and accusations of sabotage had important effects. People covered up mistakes and faults. Output figures were inflated so that industries could not be accused of failing to fulfil their targets. Workers were intimidated so that they would work harder.

How were the workers made to work so hard?

Workers in the 1930s received few rewards. Their wages were low and there were few consumer goods to buy until the end of the 1930s. Food was short and their working conditions and hours were appalling. Houses were of low standard. So how did Stalin get them to work so hard?

A better society

Many workers, especially the young, were inspired by the great task of transforming Russia. They volunteered to work on distant projects under arduous conditions. They believed in the worth of what they were doing, and were prepared to make sacrifices. They thought they were building a better society for their children.

Propaganda

A huge propaganda campaign in the cinema, on radio and in newspapers and posters was mounted to encourage people.

1. In Source 4:
   a) Who does the man in the top hat represent?
   b) Why is he laughing at the idea of the Five-Year Plan?
   c) Why has his expression changed in 1933?
   d) What was the purpose of this poster?

Awards

Awards and honours were given to individuals and groups who worked hard. Groups were also encouraged to compete against each other. One famous worker, Alexei Stakhanov, gave birth to the Stakhanovite Movement, dedicated to hard work. Stakhanov was a Donbass miner who was supposed to have moved 102 tons of coal on his own in one shift – some fourteen times the amount one man would be expected to produce. This was held up in newspapers and posters as a model for others to follow. Workers who exceeded production targets could become Stakhanovites. This entitled them to better housing, free holidays and cash prizes.

SOURCE 4   A Soviet cartoon, 1933. The sign being held up reads 'Five-Year Plan'

Wages

Wages were also used as incentives. Wages were usually paid according to how much was produced. Skilled workers could get up to four times the wages of their unskilled comrades. Those who moved up into management could get much more.

Punishments

Not all workers responded to the propaganda campaigns, and measures were introduced to deal with slackers. The fear of being accused of sabotage and sent to a labour camp encouraged workers to carry out their tasks obediently. There was also a strict code of labour discipline with tough punishments:

Was Stakhanov's story true?

SOURCE 5   A photograph of Alexei Stakhanov

The Stakhanov story was a set-up. He had two helpers who shored up the tunnel and removed the coal while he worked at the coal face with his pick. It is likely that other Stakhanovites also asked others to help them so that their tremendous achievements would be reported in newspapers.

Although they got rewards, Stakhanovites were often very unpopular with other workers, as they pushed up the production norm (the amount a worker had to produce in a shift), on which wages were calculated.

- Absenteeism was punished by fines, loss of ration cards or dismissal. By 1940, it had become a crime and a prison sentence was given for second offences.
- Workers had to carry labour books, which recorded their jobs and unfavourable comments about them. A bad record could lose a worker food rations or lead to imprisonment.

A large proportion of the workforce consisted of forced labour. These workers were made to work hard by compulsion, fear of physical punishment or being denied food. Often the really heavy work involved in constructing dams, canals and building projects – clearing sites, digging foundations – was done by prisoners, many of whom were peasants sent to labour camps as a result of COLLECTIVISATION.

■ TASK

1. Make a list of the positive ways in which workers were encouraged to increase production.
2. Which of these ways would you consider to be Socialist and which non-Socialist?
3. Why do you think that propaganda and the Stakhanovite campaign were such an important part of Stalin's methods?
4. 'Coercion and fear were the main ways Stalin got workers to work hard.' How far do you agree with this statement?

Case study: How was Magnitogorsk built?

■ SOURCE INVESTIGATION

SOURCE 1 A photograph showing an industrial plant being built at Magnitogorsk

SOURCE 2 From *The Socialist Sixth of the World*, by Johnson and Hewlett, London, 1939

❝ *On the right bank of the small river which skirted the mountains lay the Cossack village of Magnitnaya. In 1929, windswept flowery meadows lay beyond the village . . . The mountain was one vast lump of iron ore . . .*

An area of 54 square kilometres was selected for the site of Magnitogorsk. Workers of 35 nationalities assembled and built barracks for workers . . .

The attack upon the mountain began. Ledges 30 feet high were cut in it to get the ore.

Enormous structures rose; the housing of huge ore crushers . . . batteries of coke ovens and blast furnaces towering to the height of 150 feet.

The city itself is planned with care: Soviet factories turn out men as well as steel: seventeen great blocks of buildings, each with its own department store, school, restaurant, and creches; each apartment in the blocks of flats with its own bath, running water, electric light, gas and central heating.

By 1934 the mills turned out about 10 million tons of cast iron. By 1937 this had grown to 14.5 million tons. Steel production increased nine and a half times to upwards of 17.5 million tons. ❞

MAGNITOGORSK WAS a showpiece of Soviet achievement, but how was it built and what was the 'Socialist city' like?

1. a) What impression of the building of Magnitogorsk is given in Source 2?
   b) Do you think the writer was a supporter of the Soviet Union? Explain your answer.
2. a) On what points do Sources 2 and 3 agree?
   b) How is Source 3 different? Suggest reasons for this.
3. Who carried out the work at Magnitogorsk, according to Sources 2 and 3?
4. Does this suggest enthusiasm for the building of the Soviet dream?

SOURCE 3 John Scott was an American who voluntarily went to Russia to join in the building of a new country. He spent several years at Magnitogorsk. This is an extract from his book *Behind the Urals*, published in 1942

❝ *Brigades of young enthusiasts from every corner of the Soviet Union arrived in the summer of 1930 and did the groundwork of railroad and dam construction necessary. Later, groups of local peasants came to Magnitogorsk because of bad conditions in the villages, due to collectivisation. A colony of several hundred foreign engineers and specialists arrived to advise and direct the work.*

From 1928 until 1932, nearly a quarter of a million people came to Magnitogorsk. About three-quarters of these new arrivals came of their own free will, seeking work, bread cards, better conditions. The rest came under compulsion. ❞

SOURCE 4 A photograph of workers digging in Magnitogorsk

SOURCE 5   Workers looking at a board showing production plans and targets

Problems and hazards

SOURCE 6   From *Behind the Urals* by John Scott

❝Another cause of loss of working time was bad organisation of labour . . . a brigade would be sent to pour concrete foundations before the excavation work was finished. Workers would be sent to a job for which there were no materials or for which essential tools or blueprints were not available . . .

The scaffold was coated with about an inch of ice . . . besides being very slippery, it was very insecure. It swayed and shook as I walked on it . . . I was just going to start welding when I heard someone shout, and something swished past me. It was a rigger who had been working at the very top. During the entire winter of 1932–33, the riggers got no meal, no butter, and almost no sugar or milk. They received only bread and a little grain cereal.

In early April it was still bitter cold . . . everything was still frozen solid. By May, the ground had thawed and the city was swimming in mud . . . Welding became next to impossible as our ragged cables short-circuited at every step . . . Bubonic plague had broken out in three places not far from Magnitogorsk . . . The resistance of the population was very low because of undernourishment during the winter and consistent overwork. Sanitary conditions during the thaw were appalling . . . By the middle of May the heat was intolerable. In the barracks we were consumed by bed bugs and other vermin, and at work we had trouble keeping to the job. ❞

Encouragement

SOURCE 7   From *Behind the Urals* by John Scott

❝Competition between individuals, brigades and whole departments was encouraged . . . The Stakhanov movement hit Magnitogorsk in the autumn of 1935. Brigade and shop competition was intensified. Banners were awarded to the brigades who worked best, and monetary remuneration accompanied banners . . . Wages rose. Production rose.

In 1938, though the city was still in a primitive state . . . it did boast 50 schools, three colleges, two large theatres, half a dozen small ones, seventeen libraries, 22 clubs, eighteen clinics . . . a large park had been constructed in 1935.

The city of Magnitogorsk grew and developed from the dirty chaotic construction camp of the early 1930s into a reasonably healthy and habitable city. ❞

5. Using Sources 3 and 6, make a list of the problems involved in building Magnitogorsk.
6. What did Magnitogorsk consist of in 1929? What was it like by 1938?
7. Do the sources on these two pages support the statements about how industrialisation took place, made on pages 87–91? Find three examples to justify your answer.
8. How reliable do you think John Scott is as a source of evidence?

■ ACTIVITY

It is 1938. You are a Party activist who travels around industrial centres in the USSR encouraging workers. Use Sources 1–7 to write a speech about the achievements of Magnitogorsk that you will give to workers elsewhere. You can add ideas of your own using information from pages 87–91. These could include:

■ industrial achievement throughout the USSR
■ the Stakhanovite campaign
■ the problems of wreckers and saboteurs
■ the future for Soviet children.

Was industrialisation successful?

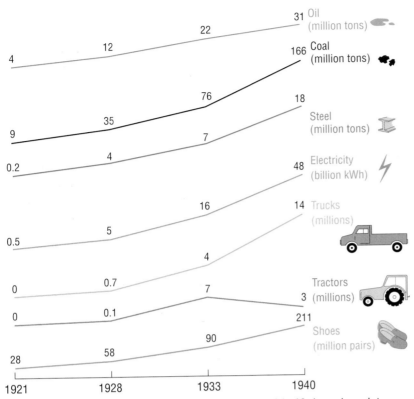

	1921	1928	1933	1940	
Oil (million tons)	4	12	22	31	
Coal (million tons)	9	35	76	166	
Steel (million tons)	0.2	4	7	18	
Electricity (billion kWh)	0.5	5	16	48	
Trucks (millions)	0	0.7	4	14	
Tractors (millions)	0	0.1	7	3	
Shoes (million pairs)	28	58	90	211	

SOURCE 1 Industrial production figures, 1921–40, based on data collected by the Soviet government

1. Do the figures in Source 1 prove that Stalin's industrialisation programme was successful?
2. How reliable is Source 2 as evidence of industrial achievement?
3. Do Sources 3 and 4, written by Western historians, support Source 2?
4. What do you think were the 'failings and shortcomings' that Westward refers to in Source 4?

■ ACTIVITY

Write an assessment of Stalin's industrialisation policy. Include in it:

■ the reasons why Stalin wanted to industrialise Russia quickly
■ whether the plans achieved his aims
■ the sort of achievements that marked the Five-Year Plans
■ the problems in the new industries
■ the price some workers had to pay for industrialisation.

Write a paragraph summing up the good and the bad points about Stalin's policy.

SOURCE 2 A Soviet view of the achievements of the second Five-Year Plan, from *History of the USSR*, by Y. Kukushkin, 1981

While the economies of the capitalist countries were sinking ever deeper into recession, the Soviet economy was booming ... The second sections of the Magnitogorsk and Kuznetsk iron and steel complexes were completed ahead of schedule. At the start of the Five-Year Plan a major victory was scored on the industrialisation front when the Urals and Novo-Kramatorsk heavy engineering plants went into operation ...

Good progress was made in constructing new railways and motorways ... 4,500 new factories, plants, mines and power stations were commissioned, three times as many as in the first Five-Year period ...

During the second Five-Year Plan period, industrial output went up by 120 per cent. The USSR moved into first place in Europe and second in the world in gross industrial output.

SOURCE 3 From *The Russian Century* by Brian Moynahan, 1995

Huge plants were built in Magnitogorsk, Chelyabinsk, Stalingrad; the giant hydroelectric scheme on the Dnieper, which quintupled Soviet electric power output ... was for two years the world's largest single construction site ... New mines were opened in Kazakhstan; heavy industry reached into Georgia. Moscow's cobbled winding lanes were replaced by broad avenues and concrete buildings, beneath which ran a subway system with marbled stations.

SOURCE 4 From *Endurance and Endeavour*, by N. Westward, 1973

The failures and shortcomings cannot disguise the fact that by 1941 the main aim of Stalin's policy of rapid industrialisation had been achieved. The USSR ... was one of the world's great industrial powers.

Why did Stalin introduce collectivisation?

IN MAY 1929, the new Five-Year Plan for agriculture announced that five million households were to be put into collective farms by 1932–33.

How were collective farms formed?

Peasants in a particular area were encouraged to put their individual plots of land together to form a collective farm or KOLKHOZ. They had to hand over their animals and tools to the farm, which would be run by a committee. The idea was that they would work together and share everything, including what the farm produced. Some of the produce would be sold to the state at a low price and, in return, the state would provide agricultural machinery such as tractors, and help the peasants to farm more efficiently.

There were other types of collective farms. In the 'toz' type, the peasants owned their own land but shared machinery. Some, called 'sovkhozes', were owned and run by the state. But the kolkhoz was the type preferred by the Communists.

Many peasants were unhappy about the idea of the kolkhoz, as Source 1 shows.

1. The peasants here put forward a number of reasons why they do not think collective farms a good idea. Write down these reasons in your own words.

Who ever heard of such a thing – to give up our land and our cows and our houses and our tools and our farm buildings, to work all the time and share everything with others?

Yes, and some woman will have ten children and will get milk for all of them; another will have only one child and will get milk for only one, and both will be doing the same work.

We won't even be sure of having enough bread to eat. Now, however poor we may be, we have our own rye and our own potatoes . . . and our own milk. We know we won't starve. But in the kolkhoz, no more potatoes of our own, no more anything of our own. Everything will be rationed by orders . . . Serfdom – that is what it is – and who wants to be a serf?

We like the feeling of independence. Today we feel like working, and we work; tomorrow we feel like lying down, and we lie down . . . We do as we please. But in the kolkhoz, brother, it is do-as-you-are-told, like a horse . . . We'll just wither away on the Socialist farm.

SOURCE 1 From *Red Bread*, by Maurice Hindus, 1931. A lot of peasants had objections to collective farms, as the author discovered when he visited the village where he used to live, in 1929

SOURCE 2   An artist's reconstruction of a collective farm or kolkhoz. Some of these were very large, with their own schools, nurseries, meeting places, dining halls and even hospitals

Why did the Communists support collectivisation?

■ Agriculture was still very backward. Most farms were small, because of the way land had been shared out after the Revolution. Old traditional methods – strip farming with wooden ploughs – were still used. Collectives made it easier to introduce modern machinery, especially tractors, and new methods of farming, which would produce more food.

■ More efficient mechanised agriculture would require fewer peasants to work the land and release the labour needed for the growing industries.

■ It was easier for the state to get grain from collective farms than from individual peasants.

■ Collectivisation was the Socialist way to farm the land. How could you build a Socialist state when peasants owned their own land and sold their produce on the private market? Collectivisation would replace capitalist attitudes with Socialist attitudes of co-operation and sharing.

SOURCE 3   Collective farms could afford to buy modern agricultural machinery, such as this harvester

SOURCE 4   Tractors were seen as the key to modern agricultural methods

Why was collectivisation so urgent?

Communist Party members were staggered by Stalin's announcement that he was going to carry out a crash collectivisation programme in four years.

The reason for this urgency lay in the food crisis of the late 1920s. Despite good harvests between 1925 and 1928, the peasants were holding back grain, because the price the state paid for it was low and they could not afford to buy much. In 1928 and 1929, matters were so bad that bread and meat had to be rationed in the cities. Stalin himself and other Party officials went out into the main grain-producing areas to seize grain. Many peasants stopped producing so much and hid supplies.

Stalin blamed the kulaks, or rich peasants, for hoarding grain, and had many arrested and deported. But he was tired of the yearly struggle to get grain which was desperately needed to feed the workers and to help pay for the industrialisation programme. Instead, he decided to break the peasants and their stranglehold on food supplies. The tool he used to do this was collectivisation.

1. Do you think the Communists had a good case for making the peasants go into collectives?
2. Why did Stalin decide to force the peasants into collectives in such a short time?
3. What consequences do you think this might have had?

SOURCE 5 (right)   Peasants looking at posters encouraging them to join a collective, 1929

SOURCE 6 (below)   Creches were provided for farm workers' babies

SOURCE 7   Soviet women learning to read at a state-run literacy class in the 1930s

SOURCE 8   A poster with the slogan 'Come and join our kolkhoz, comrade!'

4. Which of Sources 3–8 do you think were intended as government propaganda?
5. What benefits of collectivisation do they show?
6. If you were running a Communist Party newspaper, which would you use? Explain your reasons.

How was collectivisation carried out?

IN 1930, bands of Party activists and officials, backed up by the OGPU (state police), were sent into the countryside to organise the peasants into collective farms.

The activists would 'persuade' peasants to sign a register demanding to be collectivised. Then animals, implements and buildings would be taken from the kulaks (rich peasants) and would usually form the basis for the new collective farm. If the peasants refused to join the collective, they would be labelled as kulaks and shot, deported or sent to labour camps. Sometimes, whole villages were deported as a lesson to others.

'Dekulakisation' was central to the collectivisation process. It was important to have a class enemy – the kulaks – to blame for everything that went wrong. But the term 'kulak' actually meant very little by the 1930s. There were few rich peasants left: the people referred to were usually the most efficient farmers, who owned a few animals and some machinery.

However, even where kulaks did not exist, the Communists still insisted that they had to be found and cleaned out. Stalin said, 'We must liquidate the kulaks as a class.' He used class hatred to whip up hysteria. The district authorities told local Soviets how many kulaks they had to find and lists of names were drawn up. Peasants denounced others as kulaks, some to settle old scores with neighbours. Children were encouraged to inform on anybody, even their own parents.

The Soviet version

S OURCE 1   Peasants protesting against the kulaks

S OURCE 2   From *The History of the Communist Party (Short Course)*, a Soviet textbook in use in the USSR during the Stalin period

❝ The peasants chased the kulaks from the land, dekulakised them, took away their livestock and machinery, and requested the Soviet power to arrest and deport the kulaks. ❞

S OURCE 3   The official view given in the Party history published in 1960

❝ [The peasants] saw that the Party and the government, overcoming difficulties, were building factories to make tractors and new farm machines. Numerous groups of peasants visited the new factories, attended workers' meetings, and were inspired by their enthusiasm. Upon returning to their villages, the working peasantry took the initiative in setting up new collective farms. ❞

S OURCE 4   A peasant signing up for a collective farm

How others saw it

SOURCE 5   A collective farm meeting

SOURCE 6   Vasily Grossman, a Jewish Soviet writer, quoted in *The Harvest of Sorrow* by Robert Conquest

❝ *They would threaten people with guns, as if they were under a spell, calling small children 'kulak bastards', screaming 'bloodsuckers!' . . . They had sold themselves on the idea that the so-called 'kulaks' were pariahs, untouchables, vermin. They would not sit down at a 'parasite's' table; the 'kulak' child was loathsome, the young 'kulak' girl was lower than a louse. They looked on the so-called 'kulaks' as cattle, swine, loathsome, repulsive: they had no souls; they stank; they all had venereal diseases; they were enemies of the people and exploited the labour of others . . . and there was no pity for them.* ❞

SOURCE 7   A photograph of a girl informing on her parents

SOURCE 8   A kulak's description of collectivisation to John Scott, an American volunteer, quoted in *The Russian Century* by Brian Moynahan

❝ *The poor peasants of the village get together in a meeting and decide: 'So-and-so has six horses; we couldn't get along without those in the collective farm; besides, he hired a man to help him in the harvest.' They notify the OGPU, and there you are. So-and-so gets five years. They confiscate his property and give it to the new collective farm. Sometimes they ship the whole family out.* ❞

SOURCE 9   From Victor Kravchenko's book *I Chose Freedom*. Victor Kravchenko, a Communist eye-witness, arrived in a village to find a commotion

❝ *'What's happening?' I asked the constable.*
'Another round-up of kulaks,' he replied. 'Seems the dirty business will never end. The OGPU and District Committee people came this morning.'
A large crowd was gathered outside the building . . . A number of women were weeping hysterically and calling the names of husbands and fathers . . . In the background, guarded by the OGPU soldiers with drawn revolvers, stood about twenty peasants, young and old, with bundles on their backs. A few were weeping. The others stood there sullen, resigned, helpless.
So this was 'Liquidation of the kulaks as a class'! A lot of simple peasants being torn from their native soil, stripped of all their worldly goods and shipped to some distant labour camps. For some reason, on this occasion, most of the families were being left behind. ❞

1. Sources 1–4 give the Soviet version of how collectivisation was carried out. How do these sources suggest it was done?
2. How does this compare with the version in Sources 5–9?
3. In what ways do the two versions agree with each other?
4. Which version do you think is more reliable? Consider the sources individually.
5. a) How can you explain the attitudes towards the kulaks described in Source 6?
   b) Have you come across this type of abuse in other periods of history? If so, where?
6. a) How were kulaks identified?
   b) Why do you think it was so important for Stalin to present the kulaks as the enemy?

How were the peasants affected by collectivisation?

THERE WAS FIERCE resistance to collectivisation. Peasants refused to hand over their animals, preferring to slaughter them and eat or sell the meat. They burnt crops, tools and houses rather than hand them over to the state. There were also riots and armed resistance. One riot lasted five days and armoured cars were needed to put it down.

So fierce was this reaction that in March of 1930 Stalin called a temporary halt. He was worried that there would be no crop to harvest in the summer. He blamed the activists and local officials for going too far. But as soon as the harvest was gathered in, the process was begun again, a little more slowly but with just as much violence.

So much disruption was caused to agriculture that there were severe food shortages. When, added to this, there was a disastrous harvest in 1932, the result was a famine of unimaginable severity in the years 1932–33. Yet the state never admitted that a famine was taking place and did not ask for, or get, international aid. Indeed, food was still being exported from the USSR to other countries. To make matters worse, Stalin sent out requisitioning gangs to take what little grain there was. Grain was held in stores that were 'almost bursting', and even left to rot in the open while people nearby starved to death.

It has been estimated that at least thirteen million peasants, and possibly many more, died as a result of collectivisation – a human tragedy on a gigantic scale. But Stalin had succeeded in breaking the peasants and obtaining the grain he needed for industrialisation.

SOURCE 1   From Victor Serge's *Memoirs of a Revolutionary*

66 The women came to deliver the cattle confiscated by the kolkhoz, but made a rampart of their own bodies around the beasts: 'Go on, bandits, shoot!'

In a Kuban market town whose entire population was deported, the women undressed in their houses, thinking that no one would dare make them go out naked; they were driven out as they were to the cattle trucks, beaten with rifle butts...

Trainloads of deported peasants left for the icy north, the forests, the steppes, the deserts. These were whole populations, denuded of everything; the old folk starved to death in mid-journey, newborn babies were buried on the banks of the roadside, and each wilderness had its crop of little crosses. 99

SOURCE 2   In the 1930s a novel, *Virgin Soil Upturned*, was published in Russia. It was written by Mikhail Sholokhov, who was a Communist and took part in collectivisation as a Party activist. Here he writes about how the peasants reacted

66 Stock was slaughtered every night in Gremyachy Log. Hardly had dusk fallen than the muffled, short bleats of sheep, the death squeals of pigs, or the lowing of calves could be heard. Both those who had joined the kolkhoz and individual farmers killed their stock. Bulls, sheep, pigs, even cows were slaughtered, as well as cattle for breeding...

'Kill, it's not ours any more... Kill, they'll take it for meat anyway... Kill, you won't get meat on the collective farm...'

And they killed. They ate until they could eat no more. Young and old suffered from stomach ache. At dinner-time tables groaned under boiled and roasted meat. At dinner-time everyone had a greasy mouth, everyone hiccoughed as if at a wake. Everyone blinked like an owl, as if drunk from eating. 99

Here, Andrei Razmiotnov, an activist, is speaking about the brutal treatment of the peasants

66 'What am I? An executioner? Or is my heart of stone?' And he again began to shout:

'Gayev's got eleven children. How they howled when we arrived! It made my hair stand on end. We began to drive them out of the kitchen... I screwed up my eyes, and stopped my ears, and ran into the yard. The women were all in a dead fright... The children – Oh, by God, you...'

But the other chief activist would not have it:

'Snake!' he gasped in a penetrating whisper, clenching his fists. 'How are you serving the Revolution? Having pity on them? Yes... You could line up the thousands of old men, women and children and tell me they'd got to be crushed into the dust for the sake of the Revolution, and I'd shoot them all down with a machine gun.' 99

1. Use Sources 1 and 2 to explain:
■ the ways in which the peasants resisted collectivisation
■ what happened to those who resisted.
2. Why do you think this was such a bitter struggle?
3. What do Sources 2 and 5 tell you about the activists who carried out collectivisation and why they did it?
4. Source 2 is from a novel. How useful do you think it is to historians of this period?
5. a) How does Kopelev's evidence in Source 5 support the novel?
b) Do you think that the fact that he went into exile means that his account is less reliable?

SOURCE 3   Collecting the dead during the 1932 famine, probably in the Ukraine

SOURCE 4   An eye-witness account by a survivor from Viknyna (in the Kiev/Odessa region)

❝ *The poor widow Darylul and her sons had a very tragic end. Her dead body was eaten by maggots and the two sons, Pavlo and Oleska, fell dead begging for food . . .*

Oleska Voitsyskhovsky saved his and his family's lives by consuming the meat of horses which had died in the collective of glanders and other diseases. He dug them up at night and brought the meat home in a sack. **❞**

SOURCE 5   By Lev Kopelev, a party activist who later went into exile

❝ *With the rest of my generation, I firmly believed that the ends justified the means. Our great goal was the universal triumph of Communism . . .*

I saw what 'total collectivisation' meant – how they mercilessly stripped the peasants in the winter of 1932–33. I took part in this myself, scouring the countryside . . . testing the earth with an iron rod for loose spots that might lead to buried grain. With the others, I emptied out the old folk's storage chests, stopping my ears to the children's crying and the women's wails. For I was convinced that I was accomplishing the great and necessary transformation of the countryside; that in the days to come the people who lived there would be better off . . .

In the terrible spring of 1933 I saw people dying of hunger. I saw women and children with distended bellies, turning blue, still breathing but with vacant lifeless eyes. And corpses – corpses in ragged sheepskin coats and cheap felt boots; corpses in the peasant huts . . . I saw all this and did not go out of my mind or commit suicide . . . Nor did I lose my faith. As before, I believed because I wanted to believe. **❞**

6. Why has the famine of 1932–33 been described as man-made?
7. What reason could Stalin have for not taking action to relieve the suffering of the famine?

■ ACTIVITY

It is 1930.
Either
You are a Communist activist, who has been involved in 'persuading' peasants to join collective farms. You are talking to a friend of yours who works in a rural Soviet who is having doubts. Convince your friend of the importance of the success of collectivisation. Explain why it has been necessary. Mention:

■ the problems of persuading the peasants to give up their grain in the late 1920s
■ the need to deal with the capitalist kulaks
■ the benefits of collective farms
■ the importance of collectivisation to industrialisation and the Revolution.

Or
You are the friend. Explain your reservations about the way collectivisation is being carried out, especially the way in which kulaks are identified.

Did collectivisation succeed?

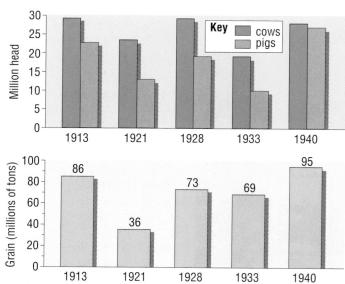

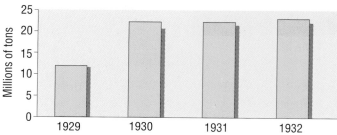

SOURCE 1 Agricultural production, based on figures produced by the Soviet government

SOURCE 2 Grain procurements (grain taken by the state)

1. a) What does the chart in Source 1 show happened to agricultural production between 1928 and 1940?
   b) How can you explain this?
   c) How does this compare with what was being produced in 1913 before the Communists came to power?
2. a) What does Source 2 show about the amount of grain that the state was able to get from the peasants even in the bad year of 1932?
   b) What did this mean for the aims of Stalin's policy?
3. How useful as evidence is Source 3 about the success of collectivisation?
4. Do you agree with the assessment of collectivisation by the two historians in Sources 4 and 5? Use evidence from this page and pages 95–103 to support your views.

■ ACTIVITY

In class, debate the statement: 'Collectivisation was a terrible disaster for the Russian people.'

SOURCE 3 Bertha Malnick visited the USSR several times during the 1930s, collecting material for her book *Everyday Life in Russia*, 1938. This extract is from a speech by the brigadier of a collective farm

"We have more than 600 hectares; of these 123 are sown with cotton, 225 planted with wheat. Our vineyards cover 45 hectares. Our three lorries can hardly cope with the work. Our farmers have built 70 new houses for themselves during the last few years . . . Look inside these houses. You will find rich carpets and musical instruments . . .

Four times [this year] the whole farm went to the opera in Erevan, to the theatre, to concerts, to the cinema . . . Look at our happy children. They all go to school. We have two schools . . . We, the older generation, dared not dream of such things . . . In our club dozens of farmers are learning to read and write, joining literary, agricultural and political classes . . .

I could say much more about the life of our collective farm, but the young wine is bubbling impatiently in your glasses. Drink to the good Stalin, who brought us to this life."

SOURCE 4 From *European History 1848–1945* by T.A. Morris

"Destruction by rebellious peasants, the loss of kulak expertise, and the inexperience of collective farm managers resulted in a sharp decline in many areas of production. Between 1928 and 1934 the cattle population of the USSR declined from 66.8 million to 35.5 million, the number of sheep and goats fell from 114.6 million to 36.5 and the number of horses from 34 million to 16.5 million. Grain shortages, combined with continued forced procurements, led to rural famine . . .

Not until 1940 did figures for grain production reach those of 1914."

SOURCE 5 From *A History of Soviet Russia*, by Adam Ulam, 1976

"Collectivisation accomplished its main aims. In the first place, the regime could now commandeer food from the peasants at incredibly low prices . . . Then it acquired the additional working force for industrialisation . . . mechanisation, especially after tractors began to be produced in quantity, released millions of rural youth for industries in the cities."

9 *HOW DID STALIN CONTROL THE USSR?*

IN THE 1930s, Stalin consolidated his position as supreme **dictator** of the Soviet Union. Stalin's USSR developed into a TOTALITARIAN state, like Adolf Hitler's Germany. A totalitarian state is one in which those in power have total control – every aspect of people's lives is controlled and monitored. The Soviet Union in the 1930s had many features in common with Nazi Germany:

- authoritarian control through terror
- secret police
- labour camps
- cult of the leader
- education controlled by the state
- propaganda and censorship
- state control of arts and sciences
- only one political party.

   In other words, Stalin maintained his powerful position in the USSR by two main methods:

- control by terror
- control of ideas.

SOURCE 1 (left)   A poster celebrating Stalin's constitution, 1937

Stalin established control over the Party and the people by a series of Purges

1934
Murder of Kirov; Stalin launches the Purges – some against ordinary people

1937
Second show trial: senior Party members executed. Purge of the army

1936
First show trial: Zinoviev and Kamenev executed

1938
Third and last show trial: Bukharin and Rykov executed. Purge of the NKVD

The Great Purges

THE 'GREAT PURGES' lasted from 1934 to 1938. During this period millions of Russians – in the Communist Party, the army, the arts and sciences, and many other walks of life – were arrested and either sent to the labour camps or shot. A feature of the purges was public show trials, where old Bolsheviks confessed to crimes against the Soviet Union.

his office in Leningrad. Stalin claimed that there was a conspiracy to murder him and destroy the Party. Using the atmosphere of fear created by the murder, he ordered arrests.

Purging the Communist Party – the show trials

SOURCE 2   A photograph of a 1930s show trial. On the right you can see Vyshinsky, the state prosecutor, who questioned the defendants

SOURCE 1   Sergei Kirov in the 1920s. At the Seventeenth Party Congress, Kirov got more applause than Stalin, a sign of his popularity

How did the purges begin?

Many Communists, especially old Bolsheviks, had been deeply disturbed by the violence of collectivisation in the early 1930s. They were shocked by the mass slaughter and human misery it had brought about. Some, including Stalin's wife, were so disillusioned that they committed suicide during the dreadful famine in 1932–33.

By 1934, when things started to improve, a large group in the Communist Party thought that it was time to slow down the drive towards industrialisation and to improve relations with the peasants. Sergei Kirov, a leading Communist, put forward these views at the Seventeenth Party Congress. There was talk of removing Stalin as leader, and Kirov seemed to be emerging as a popular alternative.

Shortly after the Congress, Kirov was shot outside

SOURCE 3   A newspaper feature put together by supporters of Trotsky in 1938, including photographs of the Central Committee of the Bolshevik Party of 1917, showing those who had become victims of Stalin

SOURCE 4   By Fitzroy MacLean, a British diplomat who observed the show trials

❝ The prisoners were charged . . . with every conceivable crime: high treason, murder, espionage and all kinds of sabotage. They had plotted to wreck industry and agriculture, to assassinate Stalin, to dismember the Soviet Union for the benefit of their capitalist allies. They were shown for the most part to have become criminals and traitors to the Soviet cause ever since the Revolution – before it, even . . . One after another, using the same words, they admitted their guilt . . . And yet what they said, the actual contents of their statements, seemed to bear no relation to reality. ❞

In 1936, Stalin set about purging (cleaning out) the Communist Party to get rid of all the people who might oppose him, particularly Bolsheviks who had been important in the past. The first to go were the old enemies – Zinoviev and Kamenev. Along with fourteen others, they were accused of organising the murder of Kirov and planning to assassinate Stalin.

They were put on trial in full view of the world, in the so-called 'show trials', which were broadcast on radio. The accused confessed to laughable charges (see Source 4), including plans to murder Lenin. The details of the evidence were even more bizarre. One of the hotels where the plotters were supposed to have met to plan the murder had been demolished years before; Smirnov, another 'plotter', had actually been in jail at the time.

Getting confessions was important. Confessions showed that the state and Stalin were right – a conspiracy did exist. It did not help the people who confessed. Zinoviev, Kamenev and the others were all executed.

The show trials were just the tip of the iceberg. Between 1936 and 1938, thousands of Communist Party members were denounced in meetings and expelled from the Party. Denouncing others was a good way to get a better job in the Party. Denunciations usually led to arrest and torture. Under torture, people often made confessions implicating others, who would then be arrested in their turn.

The second main show trial took place in 1937, when senior Party members were accused of industrial sabotage and spying. The third and last great show trial in 1938 included Bukharin, Rykov and Yagoda. It was too dangerous to have men like Bukharin around, who knew so much about the old revolutionary days. He was shot along with Yagoda,

SOURCE 5   A French cartoon showing the Communist Party consisting only of Stalin

who had been the previous head of the NKVD (secret police).

By the end of the purges of the Party, it has been estimated that over one fifth of the members had been expelled or shot. Of the 1,961 delegates at the Seventeenth Party Congress in 1934, where Kirov was clapped for longer than Stalin, 1,108 were arrested. Of the 139 Central Committee members, over 90 were shot. Five (out of eleven) of the POLITBURO of 1934 were dead, some in mysterious circumstances.

1. Why do you think so many of those who attended the Seventeenth Party Congress did not survive?
2. Why are the crimes that the prisoners were accused of (Source 4) surprising and rather strange?
3. a) What is the message of the cartoon in Source 5?
   b) Who might have produced it?
4. What do you think was the effect of the purges on the surviving members of the Communist Party?

■ ACTIVITY

Write a newspaper report about one of the show trials and the events surrounding it. Many people at the time believed the charges, but you can be a reporter who does not. Use information from pages 106–7 to help you write your article.

Who really killed Sergei Kirov?

■ SOURCE INVESTIGATION

EXACTLY WHO was responsible for the murder of Kirov remains a mystery. Look at the evidence below and see who you think did it.

The murder

At 4.00 p.m. on the afternoon of 1 December 1934, Kirov had arrived back at the Smolny, Communist Party Headquarters in Leningrad. As he approached his office, Leonid Nikolayev moved out of the shadows in the corridor and shot him in the back. Nikolayev then fainted beside the body and was arrested by the guards.

Nikolayev had been expelled from the Communist Party. He had developed a great hatred of the Party leadership and bureaucracy. He had a malformed leg, and was physically weak and subject to fits.

Who was behind the murder?

SUSPICIOUS CIRCUMSTANCES OF KIROV'S MURDER

■ The guards who were normally on the different floors of the Smolny were not there on that day.

■ Kirov's personal bodyguard, described as devoted to Kirov, did not accompany Kirov upstairs to his office. The day after the assassination, the bodyguard was killed in a car accident while being being taken for questioning by three NKVD (secret police) men. These men were completely unharmed in the accident. Not long afterwards, all three were killed.

■ Nikolayev had been arrested twice near Kirov carrying a revolver, but had been released quickly by the NKVD.

■ A new second-in-command of the NKVD had been brought to Leningrad from Moscow just before the murder. Kirov and the existing head of the NKVD, a friend of Kirov, asked Stalin to remove this man, but Stalin refused to do so.

■ After the murder, the leadership of the Leningrad NKVD were tried for negligence and sent to labour camps. However, they were treated very well, living in relative comfort and receiving gifts, until they were shot in 1937.

SOURCE 1 Kirov's body lying in state. Kirov had stood at Stalin's shoulder in the 1920s and had supported Stalin between 1930 and 1933. By 1934, he was very popular in the Party and some Communists wanted him to replace Stalin as leader

SOURCE 2 Vladimir Alliluyev, Stalin's nephew, quoted in *Stalin, a Time for Judgement* by Lewis and Whitehead, 1990

❝ Stalin had nothing to do with that murder . . . My mother was with Stalin when they phoned him and informed him that Kirov had been murdered. And my mother said to me, neither before nor after it had she ever seen Stalin in the state he was after receiving that phone call. And Stalin knew full well that this murder would be linked with his name, after the Seventeenth Congress – that was clear and understandable to him. ❞

SOURCE 3 Olga Shatunovskaya, who was on the commission which inquired into Kirov's murder, gives her opinion

❝ The NKVD latched on to this, that he [Nikolayev] was dissatisfied, and he wrote them a letter saying: 'I am ready for anything now. I hate Kirov.'

And they organised it . . . Of course, when Stalin found out that some senior Party members had asked Kirov to become leader, he decided to remove him. ❞

SOURCE 4   From Victor Serge's *Memoirs of a Revolutionary*. Serge was an oppositionist

66 *It was almost certainly an individual act committed by an enraged young Communist.* 99

SOURCE 5   Recollections of Nikita Khrushchev (Stalin's successor), published in 1989 in the Soviet magazine *Ogonyok*

66 *This murder was organised from above. I consider it was organised by Yagoda [head of NKVD], who could act only on the secret instructions of Stalin, received as they say, eye to eye.* 99

■ TASK

Use Sources 1–5 to answer the questions. Consider the reliability of each source.

1. Do you think Nikolayev did it on his own (Source 4)? Explain your answer.
2. Do you think it is likely that the NKVD were involved? Explain why.
3. Is there any evidence to link Stalin directly to the murder?
4. Who had the best motive for the murder?
5. Why is it so difficult to come to any firm conclusions about the murder?
6. What are your views about who was behind the murder?

Why did the old Bolsheviks confess?

Famous old Bolsheviks such as Zinoviev, Kamenev and Bukharin confessed to bizarre crimes against the Soviet Union. Why did they make these ludicrous confessions in front of the whole world?

1. What different reasons are suggested for the confessions in Sources 6–10?
2. Which do you think are the most likely reasons?
3. Why do you think it was so important to Stalin to get confessions from these old Bolsheviks?

SOURCE 6   From *Into the Whirlwind*, by Evgenia Ginsburg, 1968

66 *They started to work on me again. I was put on the 'conveyor belt'. The interrogators worked in shifts. I didn't. Seven days without sleep or food . . . Relaxed and fresh, they passed before me as in a dream . . .*

The object of the 'conveyor' is to wear out nerves, weaken the body, break resistance, and force the prisoner to sign whatever is required. 99

SOURCE 7   By Fitzroy MacLean, an eye-witness at the show trial of Bukharin

66 *Faced with death, he had felt the need for a cause to die for, and, for him, a lifelong Communist, there could only be one cause: the Party . . . Others had confessed for their own sakes or for the sakes of their families. His confession had been a last service to the Party.* 99

SOURCE 8   From *I was Stalin's Agent* by W.G. Krivitsky, 1939

66 *Although several factors contributed to bringing the men to the point of making these confessions, they made them at the last in the sincere conviction that this was their sole remaining service to the Party and the Revolution. They sacrificed honour as well as life to defend the hated regime of Stalin, because it contained the last faint gleam of hope for that better world to which they had consecrated themselves in early youth.* 99

SOURCE 9   From *Stalin and the Kirov Murder* by Robert Conquest, 1989

66 *Zinoviev and Kamenev were physically worn down – not by torture (though some of their juniors seem not to have been so lucky). But constant interrogation, inadequate food, overheated cells, and the failure to treat Zinoviev's liver condition began to tell.* 99

SOURCE 10   From *The Great Terror, a Reassessment* by Robert Conquest

66 *The prisoners, after some argument, finally accepted Stalin's terms, which guaranteed the lives of their supporters, and the liberty of their families. A member of Zinoviev's family told Krivitsky that one reason for capitulation was 'to save his family' and in Kamenev's case the same is obviously true.* 99

How did the purges affect the Russian people?

THE PURGES WERE not restricted to the Party. Anybody suspected of opposing Stalin was to be removed. Nobody was safe. People were taken away without warning and often never seen again. Fathers, wives, brothers and sisters simply disappeared, first to prison and then on to labour camps, usually without a trial. What crimes had these people committed? Often they never knew, or some offence would be made up, usually connected with sabotage. A railway engine driver could be arrested for driving his train too quickly or too slowly. It was not a good idea to make jokes about Stalin.

Scientists, doctors, actors, teachers, workers, all came to fear the knock on the door which announced the arrival of the secret police, the NKVD. The NKVD drove around in black cars called 'ravens'. They liked to call in the early hours of the morning. People often kept a bag packed in case the knock was for them.

Poets and writers were not trusted by Stalin. Many were arrested and treated badly. Meyerhold, a theatre director, complained that his brutal interrogator had forced him to drink his own urine and broken his left arm whilst forcing him to sign a confession with his right.

An army of informers kept the NKVD busy. Children were encouraged to inform on their parents and neighbours denounced each other. One woman was supposed to have denounced 8,000 people; the streets emptied when she came out. Pavlik Morozov, aged fourteen, denounced his own father. He was later stabbed to death by members of his family. He was held up as an example to children about how to do the 'right thing' by informing on parents disloyal to the new society. Statues of him were put up and buildings were named after him.

Informing on others was a way of proving one's loyalty – or a way of settling old scores. It was part of the hysteria which was created by the atmosphere of terror. People lived in fear of denunciation in the factory, office, farm, street and home.

SOURCE 1   The people told many stories and grim '4.00 a.m.' jokes about the purges. These are quoted in *The Russian Century* by Brian Moynahan and *Man of Steel* by Elizabeth Roberts, 1968

66 *A Moscow girl who had been out partying rang the doorbell when she came back in the early hours. Her father answered the door fully dressed, bag in hand, and slapped her face when he saw who it was. [He thought it was the secret police.]*

At four o'clock in the morning there was a knock on the door of a Moscow house which was occupied by five families. All of them leapt out of bed, but none dared to open the door . . . The knocking grew louder. Finally, one of the tenants took his courage in both hands and opened the door. He was heard whispering for a few moments . . . Then he came back to his terrified fellow tenants with a bright smile on his face. 'Nothing to worry about, comrades, the house is on fire, that's all.' **99**

1. Why do you think Stalin wanted to create this atmosphere of terror amongst the people?
2. How do you think stories and jokes like the ones in Source 1 came to be told?

SOURCE 2   Extracts from two interviews in *Stalin, A Time for Judgement*, by J. Lewis and P. Whitehead, 1990

Tamara Ter-Yegiazarova

"It became vastly more difficult to socialise because nobody knew who was informing on them . . . in the morning when you left your flat, you saw that a flat had been sealed and that those people were no longer there. Of course, your state of mind was utter terror, because nobody knew whether they would be arrested . . . People turned in on themselves."

Olga Sliozberg describes having to leave her children when she was arrested with her husband

"My son had woken up, and I said, 'Little son, get up and go to your granny – I'm going away for a while.' . . . Then I went to the little girl – she was four years old, he was six. She was sleeping with her nose in the pillow. I turned round and she started smiling. What could I do? I kissed her and left."

The purges of the armed forces

Stalin wanted to make sure that the army remained loyal and that any officers capable of opposing him were removed. In 1937, Marshal Tukhachevsky, along with seven other generals, all 'Heroes of the Civil War', were executed. It was also another act of personal revenge for Stalin: Tukhachevsky had had serious disagreements with Stalin in the Civil War. In the following months, thousands of army officers shared their fate. The navy and the airforce were also purged.

The consequences of this were almost disastrous for the Soviet Union. So many top army officers were removed, including 90 per cent of all Soviet generals, that the Russian army found itself in a desperate situation at the beginning of the Second World War in 1941.

■ TASK

What were the main consequences of the purges for the Soviet Union? Look back through this section before you answer. Include comments on the following:
■ how Stalin's political position had changed
■ what had been lost – people, ideas, artistic work
■ what had happened to the Communist Party
■ what had happened to the army
■ how people's lives were affected.

The end of the purges

In 1938, Stalin called a halt to the purges. Things were getting out of hand. The purges had developed a power of their own and were pulling Soviet society apart. As usual, Stalin blamed others for the excesses, though in this case it was probably true. The NKVD itself was now purged so that its knowledge of what had happened could be conveniently forgotten. It is said that the agents faced torture and death with remarkable calm.

Soviet historians have estimated that by 1939 over twenty million Russians had been transported to labour camps, and that approximately twelve million of these died. Mass graves of people killed in the 1930s have been found. A grave discovered at Chelyabinsk in the Urals in 1989 contained the bodies of more than 80,000 people.

As a result of the terror, Stalin's position was unchallengeable. He had created a Party which was composed of men and women totally loyal to him, who carried out his orders and had no memory of the old heroes of the Revolution. Moreover, all sources of opposition outside the Party had been crushed.

SOURCE 3   The mass grave at Chelyabinsk being excavated

Why did Stalin carry out the purges?

Did Stalin start the purges because he was power mad? Was he a cruel tyrant suffering from paranoia? Or were there other reasons?

As we have seen, Stalin's position as leader was under threat in 1934 (see page 106). There had been calls for his removal and many Communists wanted to build better relations with the people.

Stalin, for his part, was convinced that he was the only person who could transform the Soviet Union into a modern, industrialised country, and that it had to be done quickly. He was obsessed by the idea that Hitler would attack the USSR and that it would lose the war if it could not produce enough armaments. To slacken the pace of industrialisation, therefore, would be a betrayal of the Soviet Union. Any person who tried to stop him accomplishing this great task was, in Stalin's eyes, a traitor. Historians and others have given various reasons for the purges.

1. The official Soviet version of the purges is given in Source 4.
a) Why were the purges necessary according this version?
b) How useful is this version to historians studying Soviet history?
2. a) What role, according to Sources 5 and 6, did Stalin's personality and psychology play in this?
b) How far can we rely on Bukharin's and Khrushchev's opinions?
3. What evidence can you find in this section to support Isaac Deutscher's statement in Source 7?

■ ACTIVITY

Write a short essay on why Stalin carried out the purges. Use all the information on pages 106–12. Mention:

■ the situation in 1934
■ why Stalin thought it was important he remain leader
■ why he wanted to get rid of the old Bolsheviks
■ the role of terror in controlling the Party and the people
■ other factors, including his personality and psychology.

SOURCE 4   From *A Short History of the USSR* by A.V. Shestakov, 1938, the official Soviet history book written for students

66 *Trotsky and his contemptible friends . . . organised in the USSR gangs of murderers, wreckers and spies. They caused train collisions in the USSR, blew up and set fire to mines and factories, wrecked machines and poisoned workers, and did all the damage they possibly could. These enemies of the people had a definite programme, which was to restore the yoke of the capitalists and the landlords to the USSR, to destroy the collective farms . . . and to promote the defeat of the USSR in the event of war.* 99

SOURCE 5   Bukharin speaking in Paris in 1936

66 *He [Stalin] is convinced that he is greater than everyone else . . . If someone speaks better than he does, that man is for it! Stalin will not let him live, because that man is a constant reminder that he, Stalin, is not the first and best . . . he is a narrow-minded, malicious man – no, not a man, but a devil.*

Later he said in a letter to a friend:

Old Bolsheviks rejected Stalin in the depths of their hearts, old Bolsheviks would betray him at the first change in the political atmosphere. 99

SOURCE 6   From Nikita Khrushchev's Secret Speech, 1956. Khrushchev became leader of the Soviet Union after Stalin

66 *Stalin was a very distrustful man, sickly suspicious . . . He could look at a man and say: 'Why are your eyes so shifty today?' or 'Why are you turning so much today and avoiding looking me directly in the eyes?' The sickly suspicion created in him a general distrust even toward eminent Party workers whom he had known for years. Everywhere and in everything he saw 'enemies', 'double dealers' and 'spies'.* 99

SOURCE 7   Adapted from *Stalin*, by Isaac Deutscher, 1949

66 *Stalin's real motive was to destroy the men who might form an alternative government.* 99

What were the labour camps like?

THE LABOUR CAMPS were at the centre of Stalin's programme of terror. People feared being sent to them almost as much as being shot. Few survived the harsh conditions there. The camps were found all around the Soviet Union, but some of the worst were in the frozen north, where conditions were severe in the extreme.

In the late 1920s and early 1930s, labour camps took the peasants accused of being kulaks or who resisted collectivisation and the workers accused of sabotage and 'wrecking'. These people were often used as forced labour to clear ground for industrial towns or for big projects such as the building of the Belomar Canal. After the purges began, the camps filled up with political prisoners. There were also women's and children's camps.

SOURCE 2   Forced labourers building the Belomar Canal in 1931

What was it like in the camps?

SOURCE 1   These letters were sent by people who were put in the camps because of their religious faith

> From the Urals
> 1 February 1931
> Dear . . . . . . ,
> It is impossible to describe the need, grief, pain and humiliation which we are suffering here.
>
> Everyone is forced to work, from the age of twelve to 70 and over, in fact everyone who is still able to stand on his feet; some of them are even taken from their sick beds. They wanted to take one man by force and refused to believe he was ill, and the same evening he died, leaving a sick wife with three children.

> From 'R' in North Russia
> 18 February, 1931
> My dear sister,
> Received your letter with many thanks, and am longing for another sign of life from you . . . Eighty per cent are already unable to work. Numbers of them have frozen hands and feet. Many run away from the work as they have no warm clothing and are starving. When caught, they are locked up and have to lie on the cold ground without food, and thus they remain until the Almighty releases them from this world.
>
> Many die of hunger in the woods and are simply buried in the snow without clothing. Some are seen lying on the road too weak to move. Try to work day and night on 300 grams of bread a day, without rest! Drops of our blood are on every log. In our barracks we have eleven cases of typhoid, and no medicine.

SOURCE 3   Extracts from *Eleven Years in Soviet Prison Camps*, by Elinor Lipper, 1951

Meals

66 Breakfast: Half a herring or 50 grams of salt fish, sweetened tea; one third of the bread ration [300–850 grams].
Lunch: Cabbage-leaf soup, one pint. Groats. One third of the bread ration.
Supper: Cabbage-leaf soup, with a few grains of some cereal and fish heads floating in it. One third of the bread ration. 99

Bugs

66 The barracks were so overrun with bed bugs that sleep was almost impossible at night, when the creatures are most active. From the walls and the planks above and beneath us, they came crawling; they fell on the tormented bodies of the prisoners, who twisted and writhed at the stinging bites. 99

Rape

66 The guard who was supposed to take her back to the women's camp had not yet come. The men, of course, hastened to pay her compliments, and invited her back to their barracks . . . A few men stood as lookouts . . . the others fell on her . . . After a while, she learned she had contracted both syphilis and gonorrhoea. Her experience was not unique in Kolyma. 99

SOURCE 4   From *Into the Whirlwind* by Evgenia Ginzburg, 1968

" The camp consisted of a huge, dirty yard surrounded by barbed wire; it stank intolerably of ammonia and chloride of lime, which was forever being poured down the latrines. A special breed of bugs infested the long wooden huts . . .

Before dawn we were marched to a bleak open field. Until 1.00 p.m. we hacked at the frozen soil with spades. We ate between 1.00 p.m. and 1.30 at the camp, trying to warm ourselves over the stove. From 1.30 until 8.00 p.m. we worked again. "

■ ACTIVITY

You are a political prisoner who has been to several labour camps. You are desperate to smuggle out a report to the rest of the world to tell people what is happening in the USSR. Use Sources 1–5 to write your report on life in the labour camps. Mention:

■ daily life
■ the work you have to do
■ the conditions of work
■ food
■ accommodation
■ the behaviour of the guards.

SOURCE 5   Alexander Solzhenitsyn wrote a novel, *One Day in the Life of Ivan Denisovich*, which was based on the eleven years he spent in prison and camps

" As usual, at five o'clock that morning reveille was sounded by the blows of a hammer on the length of rail hanging up near the staff quarters . . . everything outside still looked like the middle of the night when Ivan Denisovich Shukhov got up to go to the bucket . . . "

Food

" [Shukhov's bread was handed to him.] A spoonful of granulated sugar lay in a small mound on top of the hunk . . . he sucked the sugar from the bread with his lips . . . and looked at his ration, weighing it in his hand and hastily calculating if it reached the regulation 55 grams . . . There was short weight in every ration. The only point was how short . . .

The little fish were more bone than flesh; the flesh had been boiled off the bone and had disintegrated, leaving a few remnants on head and tail. Shukhov went on champing his teeth and sucking the bones, spitting the remains on the table. He ate everything – the gills, the tail, the eyes when they were still in their sockets . . .

After . . . there was magara porridge. It had grown cold too, and had set into a solid lump . . . it was tasteless when hot, and left you with no sense of having filled your belly. "

Going to work

" Once beyond the camp boundary, the intense cold, accompanied by a head wind, stung Shukhov's face . . .

The chief of the escort recited the 'morning prayer', which every prisoner was heartily sick of:

'Attention, prisoners. Marching orders must be strictly obeyed. Keep to your ranks. No hurrying, keep a steady pace. No talking. Keep your eyes fixed ahead and your hands behind your backs. A step to the right or left is considered an attempt to escape and the escort has orders to shoot without warning. Leading guards, quick march.'

From time to time one of the escorts would cry: 'U 48. Hands behind back', or 'B 502. Keep up.' "

Work

" They'd been given the job of pecking out holes in the ground. The holes were small enough . . . but the ground, stone hard even in summer, was now in the grip of frost . . . They went for it with picks – the picks slipped, scattering showers of sparks, but not a bit of earth was dislodged. "

Parcels

" Every time someone in the team, or close by in the barracks, received a parcel (which was almost every day) his heart ached because there wasn't one for him . . .

Guards opened the parcels . . . They took out everything and examined the contents . . . If there was anything home-baked, or some tasty sweetmeats . . . the guard would take a bite at it himself . . . Every zek [prisoner] who got a parcel had to give and give, starting with the guard who opened it. "

How did Stalin control ideas?

TERROR AND PROPAGANDA were two of the chief ways in which Stalin controlled ideas in the Soviet Union. People were too frightened to speak out against the state, because someone might report them to the secret police. Stalin mounted a huge propaganda campaign in posters, films, radio, books and newspapers (all of which were state-controlled) to push the government's views.

The arts

Stalin regarded writers and artists as dangerous. Writers were censored: their books and articles had to be submitted to committees before they were published. They had much less freedom under Stalin than they had in the 1920s. Artists were forced to produce work which glorified the achievements of Soviet workers and peasants, or of the Revolution. This was called 'Socialist Realism'. Sources 1 and 2 are examples of Socialist Realist paintings. Socialist Realist novels had as their heroes ordinary people helping to build the new Soviet society.

Any work other than this was called 'BOURGEOIS'. Writers and artists accused of bourgeois tendencies would find that their work was never published or seen. They might lose their livelihood, as the state paid their wages. If they went too far, as Osip Mandelstam did when he wrote a poem critical of Stalin (see Source 3), they would find themselves in a labour camp.

Some artists, so depressed by what had happened in the USSR, left the country or committed suicide.

You can see other examples of Socialist Realist paintings on pages 117 and 119.

SOURCE 1   A painting entitled *Higher and Higher*, 1934

SOURCE 2   A painting entitled *A Collective Farm Harvest Festival*, 1937

1. What impression of Soviet society are the artists of Sources 1 and 2 trying to put across?
2. Compare the Socialist Realist paintings in Sources 1 and 2 with the art of the post-Revolution 1920s on pages 70–73.
a) What are the main differences?
b) What are the similarities?
3. Why do you think Stalin wanted to make all art and literature follow the Socialist Realism line?

115

SOURCE 3   An extract from Osip Mandelstam's poem about Stalin

"All we hear is the Kremlin mountaineer
The murderer and peasant-slayer
His fingers are fat as grubs
And the words, final as lead weights, fall from his lips,
His cockroach whiskers leer
And his boot tops gleam.
Around him a rabble of thin-necked leaders –
Fawning half-men for him to play with
They whinny, purr or whine
As he prates and points a finger "

SOURCE 4   From Victor Serge's *Memoirs of a Revolutionary*

"Censorship in many forms, mutilated or murdered books. Before sending a manuscript to the publisher, an author would assemble his friends, read his work to them and discuss together whether such-and-such pages would 'pass'. The head of the publishing enterprise would then consult the Glavlit, or Literature Office, which censored manuscripts and proofs. Once the book was published, official critics would issue their opinion . . . whether it would be tolerated, or whether it would be withdrawn from publication. "

Education

Education was strictly controlled. In the 1920s, old forms of discipline and examinations had been abolished. But this created unruly, poorly educated pupils. In 1932, a rigid programme of education was introduced. Discipline was strict and examinations were brought back.

What was taught in schools was laid down by the government. History was particularly important, and as the 1930s went on it was rewritten to suit Stalin. As the old Communists were purged, their pictures were pasted out of the textbooks. Trotsky disappeared early on, and later generations of Soviet children knew little about him. Stalin had a new book, *A Short History of the USSR*, written for school students, which gave him a more important role in the Revolution.

Outside school, children joined political youth groups, which trained them in Socialism. Children aged eight to ten joined the Octobrists, and those aged ten to sixteen joined the Pioneers. Young people aged nineteen to twenty-three joined the Komsomol. These groups were taught political ideas through activities such as sports, camping, model-making and so on.

The Church

Attacks on the Orthodox Church and religious ideas increased in the 1930s. The 'League of the Godless' smashed churches and burned religious pictures. Members of religious groups, such as the Baptists, were arrested in large numbers and sent to labour camps (see Source 1 on page 113). The Orthodox Church was hit harder as the purges continued, with most of its bishops being arrested. Trying to spread religious ideas was a passport to prison.

1. a) What is Osip Mandelstam's poem saying?
b) Did he deserve to be put in a labour camp for it?
2. a) How were books censored (see Source 4)?
b) What kind of books would not be 'passed'?

■ ACTIVITY

Discuss the following questions in class:

1. Why do some governments today, and in the past, worry about the ideas of artists, poets and writers?
2. Why is education, especially the history children are taught, so important if you want to control a society?

The cult of personality

ONE OF THE features of totalitarian societies is the glorification of the leader as an almost god-like super-being. This is called the 'cult of the personality'. A huge propaganda machine pushed the cult of Stalin into every corner of the workplace, street and home. Huge parades in Red Square in Moscow, films, statues and paintings all proclaimed the good fortune of the Soviet people in having Stalin to guide and care for them.

1. Look at the images of Stalin in Sources 1–4. Describe how he is presented in each source. Refer to details in the source to explain your answer.

SOURCE 1   The cover of *Ogonyok* magazine, December 1949, showing Stalin as a god-like figure in the sky

SOURCE 2   A poem printed in *Pravda* in 1935

" O great Stalin, O leader of the peoples,
Thou who broughtest man to birth . . .
Thou who makest bloom the spring,
Thou who makest vibrate the musical chords . . .
Thou, splendour of my spring, O thou,
Sun reflected by millions of hearts. "

SOURCE 3   A poster showing Stalin thanking Soviet youth

SOURCE 4   A painting of Stalin with industrial workers

SOURCE 5 From an interview with Alexander Avdeyenko, quoted in *Stalin, A Time for Judgement*, by J. Lewis and P. Whitehead

❝*Looking back on my life, I now see that period as one of sincere enthusiasm, of genuine happiness, and yet, at the same time, of self-hypnosis . . . from the personality cult of Stalin. It was impossible to withstand . . . the pressure which was put on people's reason, heart and soul. Day and night, radio told us that Stalin was the greatest man on earth – the greatest statesman, the father of the nation, the genius of all time . . . Man wants to believe in something great.* ❞

1. What effect did the propaganda have on young Russians (Sources 5 and 6)?
2. How does Source 5 account for the success of the propaganda?
3. What do you think is the purpose of creating the 'cult of the personality'?

Changing history

Stalin had got rid of the old Communists, who knew about the past. They were now 'enemies of the people'. He could not admit that they had been 'Heroes of the Revolution'. So history was rewritten

SOURCE 6 Pavel Litvinov, a schoolboy at the time, quoted in *Stalin, A Time for Judgement*, by J. Lewis and P. Whitehead

❝*Stalin was like a God for us. We just believed he was an absolutely perfect individual, and he lived somewhere in the Kremlin, a light always in his window, and he was thinking about us, about each of us. That was how we felt. For example, somebody told me that Stalin was the best surgeon. He could perform a brain operation better than anyone else, and I believed it. I knew that he was busy with other things, but if he wanted to do it he would be better.* ❞

and photographs were doctored so that these people disappeared from Soviet history.

At the same time, Stalin wanted Russians to think that he had been the most important person, after Lenin, in planning and carrying out the Revolution. He wanted to associate himself with Lenin, who was treated like a god in Soviet society. Stalin encouraged the 'cult of Lenin', and had paintings done to show how close to Lenin he had been in the revolutionary days.

4. Look at Source 7. Which of these two photos would Stalin not allow to be used in books? Explain why.

SOURCE 7 Two photographs of Lenin addressing a crowd. The photos were taken within seconds of each other

S OURCE 8   A photograph taken in April 1925

S OURCE 9   The same photograph, published in
the Soviet Union fourteen years later

5. Compare the photographs in Sources 8 and 9. What has changed and why?
6. What does this tell you about the use of photographs as evidence in history?
7. Why would Stalin want the images of him in Sources 10 and 11 (he is to the right of Lenin) to be shown to the Russian people?
8. The process of changing history continued under later Soviet leaders. What has happened to Stalin in Source 12? Why?

■ ACTIVITY

Discuss the following questions in class:

1. Why are visual images so important in history and society?
2. What do they do that words cannot?

S OURCE 10   Stalin has been added to this 1922
photo of Lenin

S OURCE 11   A Socialist Realist painting of Lenin
addressing workers, soldiers and sailors during the
Revolution, painted by V. Serov in the 1940s

S OURCE 12   Painted by Serov in the 1950s, after Stalin's
death

What was daily life like in the mid-1930s?

LIFE WAS NOT bad for everybody in the 1930s. For some there had been a marked improvement since Tsarist times and the early revolutionary period, even if some early ideas were abandoned. Many people believed in Stalin and went about their daily lives convinced they were building a better society. They shared many of Stalin's hopes and values.

The changing role of women

By the mid-1930s, some of the more liberal ideas – free love, easy abortion and divorce – of the early 1920s had been abandoned and the family was back in favour. The upheavals of the early 1930s and the very high divorce rate had created a vast army of homeless children, who lived on the streets, begged and robbed passers-by. The state now encouraged families to stay together through propaganda (see Source 5).

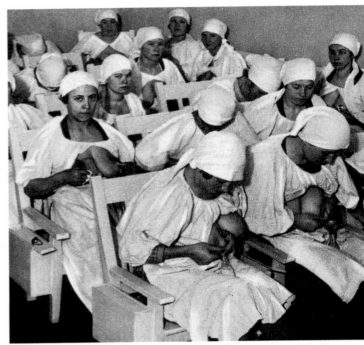

SOURCE 2   Women expressing milk at a factory. Their babies could be given the milk while the women worked

SOURCE 1   A poster with the slogan: 'The wide development of a network of creches, kindergartens, canteens and laundries will ensure the participation of women in Socialist reconstruction'

SOURCE 3   Soviet pilots in the 1930s

SOURCE 4 Children at a state-run kindergarten in the 1930s

SOURCE 5 From *Pravda* (the Party newspaper), 28 May 1936

66 *When we talk of strengthening the Soviet family we mean the fight against [the wrong] attitudes towards marriage, women and children. 'Free love' and a disorderly sex life have nothing in common with Socialist principles or the normal behaviour of a Soviet citizen . . . The outstanding citizens of our country, the best of Soviet youth, are almost always devoted to their families.* 99

They also paid child allowances for married couples. Divorce was made much harder, and restrictions were placed on abortion. Ceremonial marriages also made a comeback.

On the work front, the gains made by women in the Revolution were maintained. Women were now on a much more equal footing with men, able to gain jobs in all fields. There were demands for even more support to enable them to work, as in Source 1. Towards the end of the 1930s, however, more 'feminised' images replaced those of shock-worker women.

1. What do Sources 1–4 tell us about attitudes towards women in Soviet society?
2. What view of sex and the family was *Pravda* promoting in 1936 (Source 5)?
3. a) What views about abortion are given in Source 6?
b) Which view is closer to the ideas about abortion after the Revolution?

SOURCE 6 Extracts from letters to magazines at the time of the new abortion law, May 1936

From Tatanya Koval of the Lubchenko collective farm, Kiev district

66 *I can't find words to express my gratitude to the Party and the Government, to dear Comrade Stalin for his care of us women. I have seven children . . . My children are my joy. I've never had an abortion, and I'm not going to have any. I've borne children and shall go on bearing them.* 99

From Nina Ershova, Moscow

66 *If a mother has seven children one has to be sent to school, another to the kindergarten, the third to a creche; and then in the evening Mother has to collect them all, give them supper, look after their clothes, put them to bed . . . Well, then, that mother won't have much time left for work – in fact, she won't have a single minute left to herself. This surely means that women will be unable to take part in public life, unable to work . . .*

This new law undoubtedly has much in its favour, but it is still too early to talk of prohibiting abortion. We must first further develop our communal restaurants so that a woman shall not have to bother about dinners, suppers and breakfast . . . We must have more and better creches and kindergartens, more laundries . . . 99

Living standards

Living standards rose in the mid-1930s, but there were still shortages of food and other goods. Some Russians were doing quite well in the new system, especially high-ranking Party officials, skilled factory workers and peasants, who could get high prices for food grown on their private plots. There were great differences in wages.

The government put a lot of resources into building a health service, although the demands on it were overwhelming. It was very rigid, with people being forced to do as they were told (including having operations that were not required), but there was a great increase in facilities and doctors.

SOURCE 7 Patients at a government-built sanatorium in the 1930s

SOURCE 8 The interior of an apartment inhabited by better-off Russians in the 1930s

SOURCE 9 From *Back from the USSR*, by the French novelist André Gide, 1936

66 *I visited several dwellings in this highly prosperous farm. I wish I could convey the queer depressing impression produced by each of these 'homes' – the impression of complete depersonalisation. In each, the same ugly furniture, the same portrait of Stalin, and absolutely nothing else, not the smallest object, not the smallest personal souvenir.* 99

Housing

Housing remained a problem, and there was little overall improvement: in Moscow, only six per cent of households had more than one room. However, there was some progress in the new industrial towns by the end of the decade.

SOURCE 10 A description of a Moscow apartment house by Freda Utley, from *Lost Illusion*, 1949

66 *Badly built, with doors and windows of unseasoned wood which would not shut properly, unpapered and thinly whitewashed walls, these two rooms were home . . . By American and British standards, we were living in a squalid tenement house. But by Soviet Russian standards we were housed almost like Communist aristocrats. We not only had two rooms to live in, but we had the luxury of gas for cooking instead of a smelly oil stove. And best of all we had a bathroom with a lavatory, which we had to share with only one other family . . .* 99

Leisure

Another area in which life improved was leisure. Sport and fitness were encouraged to improve the general health of Soviet men and women. Every worker was entitled to take a holiday each year – holidays had been unknown for ordinary Russians before the Revolution. Trade unions and collective farms played a big role in providing clubs, sports facilities, film shows, festivals and general entertainments.

SOURCE 11 From John Scott's *Behind the Urals*, 1942

66 *Magnitogorsk had ten theatres with a total seating capacity of 9,000, all attached to various clubs . . . the activities of these clubs were varied and included dramatic circles, classes, sports circles, chess and checkers, art and literary groups . . . Ballroom dancing in 1935 became a popular phase of club activities . . . We went to the movies in the cinema palace, the so-called 'Magnit' which seated about 1,000. About 20,000 people attended the cinema per month.* 99

SOURCE 12 Extracts from the summer programme of the Gorky Park of Culture and Rest in Moscow

Physical culture
Sports stadium, training ground for acrobatics, volleyball, basketball and tennis, table games, wrestling and boxing rings, weight-lifting. Swimming school open from 10.00 a.m. to 8.00 p.m.

Children's section
'Archimedes' club for child inventors from twelve to eighteen years. Young Naturalists' club. Hall of Interesting Occupations. Table-games Club. Toy Pavilion. Children's autovelodrome [a spinning car for practice in balancing]. Pedal motorcars and bicycles. Races and car games.

Lenin Hills section
Bathing beach – open from 10 a.m. to 10 p.m. Sunbathing . . . beach chairs, games and diversions. Gymnastics – doctor in attendance. Boats and canoes.

Theatres, etc.
Dramatic theatre – plays under direction of H.P. Khmelev. Visit of the Saratov Dramatic Theatre. Children's music hall. Cinema and newsreel theatre.

SOURCE 13 A Leningrad café in 1937

1. In what ways had living standards improved in the Soviet Union?
2. a) What, according to Source 10, was the quality of housing like?
   b) Why do you think that housing was still a problem?
3. a) Did everybody have the same quality of housing?
   b) How did people get better living accommodation?
4. What types of leisure activities did Russians enjoy in the 1930s?
5. Do you think the lives of many ordinary people in Soviet Russia had improved since the Revolution?
   a) You could draw up a chart to help you answer this question. Things you could compare are: work, the role of women, clothes, housing, health, education, leisure activities.
   b) Write down your conclusions: in what ways had things got better and in what ways had they got worse?

■ ACTIVITY

It is 1937. You have come to the USSR on a visit from Britain as part of a trade union delegation, to look at life in the new Socialist society. You have to give a talk entitled 'Life in the Soviet Union today' when you return home. Write the notes which you will use to give the talk. Then choose three pictures to illustrate your talk and write detailed captions for each one. Use Sources 1–13 and the other information in this section to help you.

chapter 10

CONCLUSION

Was Stalin a disaster for the Soviet Union?

STALIN HAS been called the 'gravedigger of the Revolution'. This means that he spoiled everything the original revolutionaries hoped to achieve in 1917 when they started to build the new Socialist society. He is blamed for turning Russia into a totalitarian state and condemned as a mass murderer.

Some historians, however, say that he was simply carrying on the work of Lenin who had ruled Russia ruthlessly, introducing the Cheka and labour camps. Stalin, they say, simply took things further. Many Russians point to Stalin's achievements, how he turned Russia into a modern industrialised country. They claim that this could not have been achieved without Stalin's drive and determination.

Here are some points that have been made for and against Stalin:

SOURCE 1   A photograph of Stalin supposedly signing death warrants

Against Stalin

■ He caused the deaths of millions of people during collectivisation and the purges.

■ He got rid of some of the Soviet Union's best brains – thinkers, writers, artists – who could have produced brilliant work in many fields.

■ He destroyed the Communist Party, turning it into an organisation for carrying out his orders. He got rid of the old Communists who might have been able to steer the Soviet Union towards a more humane form of Socialism.

■ He was responsible for 30 years of terror and fear, turning Russia into a totalitarian state.

■ Collectivisation was not successful despite the terrible upheaval.

■ Living standards did not go up much. Housing, in particular, remained poor.

In favour of Stalin

■ He turned Russia into a powerful, modern industrial nation in 30 years.

■ He did not personally order all the excesses of the purges. The secret police got out of control.

■ There were advances in medicine and education. Enormous numbers of people learned to read and write.

■ Living standards were beginning to rise.

■ His policy of forced industrialisation saved Russia in the Second World War. They had the arms, planes and tanks they needed to fight Hitler.

■ His strong leadership helped the Soviet Union to win the Second World War.

SOURCE 2   From G.F. Alexandrov, *Joseph Stalin, a Biography*, 1947. This was an official biography, published in Moscow while Stalin was still alive

66 J.V. Stalin is a genius, the leader and teacher of the Party, the great guide of the Soviet State and captain of its armies . . . his energy truly amazing. Everyone is familiar with . . . the crystal clarity of his mind, his iron will, his devotion to the Party . . . and love for the people. 99

SOURCE 3   From Walter Duranty, *I Write As I Please*, 1935. Duranty was an American journalist who worked in Russia

66 Looking backwards over the fourteen years I have spent in Russia, I cannot escape the conclusion that this period has been a heroic chapter in the life of Humanity. During these years the first true Socialist State . . . was constructed and set moving despite incredible difficulties. . . . The USSR is now economically and financially independent; it has the largest and perhaps most powerful army in Europe; it has vast territory and resources, which it is learning to develop and use. In short, the USSR has recovered the position lost by the Tsarist Empire in 1917.

Am I wrong in believing that Stalin is the greatest living statesman? . . . Stalin and his associates have carried with them the strongest elements of the Russian people, and have created a national unity and enthusiasm which the Tsarist Empire never knew. 99

SOURCE 4   From Stephen Cohen, *An End to Silence*, 1982

66 The accomplishments cannot be lightly dismissed. During the first decade of Stalin's leadership . . . a mostly backward, agrarian, illiterate society was transformed into a predominantly industrial, urban and literate one. For millions of people, the 1930s were a time of willingly heroic sacrifice, educational opportunity, and upward mobility. 99

SOURCE 5   Svetlana Alliluyeva, Stalin's daughter, in her book *Only One Year*, published in 1969 when she was living in the United States

66 He gave his name to this bloodbath of absolute dictatorship. He knew what he was doing. He was neither insane nor misled. With cold calculation he cemented his own power, afraid of losing it more than anything else in the world. And so his first concentrated drive had been the liquidation of his enemies and rivals. The rest followed later. 99

SOURCE 6   A French cartoon, 1935. The placard says, 'We are perfectly happy'

1. What, according to Sources 2, 3 and 4, had Stalin achieved as leader of the Soviet Union?
2. a) Would you describe Source 2 as a reliable source?
   b) What words and phrases in Source 3 suggest that Duranty is sympathetic to Stalin and the Soviet way of life?
   c) What does Duranty not mention?
3. Explain how Sources 1, 5, 6 and 7 present a different view of Stalin.
4. Examine Sources 2, 5 and 6. Which do you think is the most reliable and useful for historians? Explain your answer by referring to all three sources.

SOURCE 7 Adam Ulam, *Stalin the man and his Era*, 1974

❝ He was corrupted by absolute power. Absolute power turned a ruthless politician into a monstrous tyrant. The terror was necessary, not only to keep men obedient, but even more to make them believe. ❞

SOURCE 9 From M. McCauley, *Stalin and Stalinism*, 1983

❝ It is my belief that Stalin was a very skilled, indeed gifted, politician, and one of the great figures of the twentieth century. This does not mean that that he was a good man. He had a dark and evil side to his nature. ❞

SOURCE 8 Nikita Khrushchev, in a speech at the 20th Party Congress, 1956

❝ Stalin was convinced that this [the use of terror and executions] was necessary for the defence of . . . the interests of the victory of Socialism and Communism . . . He considered this should be done in the interests of the Party; of the working masses, in the name of the defence of the Revolution's gains. In this lies the whole tragedy! ❞

1. a) In what ways do Sources 8 and 9 help explain why Stalin acted as he did?

b) Do they give a more balanced view of Stalin?

■ **ACTIVITY**

Was Stalin a disaster for the USSR?

Divide a page into two columns as opposite:

Use the information and sources here to make points for and against Stalin. You must also find evidence to support your points. You can find this in other parts of this book, in particular, the assessments of Stalin's economic policies and the sections on how he controlled Soviet Russia.

When you have collected enough evidence, write your assessment of Stalin. Each point and supporting evidence should form one paragraph in your piece of writing. In the last paragraph, write your own conclusions about Stalin.

Stalin was a disaster for the USSR	Stalin was good for the USSR

■ TASK

Was Stalin a new tsar?

Stalin has often been compared to the tsars who ruled Russia before the Revolution. Some historians say that Stalin had the same sort of power as a tsar and ruled in a similar way.

1. Compare Stalin with the tsars on the features listed below. Add any other points you can think of.

2. Discuss the following questions.

a) How similar/different was Stalin's control of Russia to that of the tsars? Would you describe him as a 'tsar'?

b) Do you think the nature of Russia (size, communications, different nationalities) required a strong, centralised, authoritarian leader to run it?

SOURCE 10 (right)   A French poster of the 1930s

Features of tsars' control of Russia	Stalin's control of USSR
Rule by one person (autocrat) who made key decisions	
Power of life and death over subjects	
No democracy. Tsar did not have to consult a parliament before making decisions	
Ordinary people's views not represented or listened to	
Tsar seen as father figure looking after Russian people	
Tsar's position justified by religious beliefs. Put there by God and had godlike qualities	
Orders carried out by an army of bureaucrats who did what they were told without question	
Secret police dealt with any opposition	
Political opponents or government critics imprisoned or sent to Siberia	
Limited freedom of speech	
Press censored	
Political parties illegal	

Glossary

autocrat a ruler with complete and absolute power

Bolshevik a member of one of the groups formed after the split of the Social Democratic Party in 1903 (*see* **Menshevik**). This group was led by Lenin. They believed that a small party of revolutionaries should seize power when the time was right

bourgeois middle-class; often used in a negative sense by the Soviets, for example to refer to ideas or art which they regarded as anti-revolutionary

capitalist owner of the means of creating wealth, for example a landowner or factory owner

censor to ban or cut portions of a newspaper, book, film, etc., often those which the government finds politically unacceptable

collectivisation the process introduced by Stalin whereby individuals' land and farms were put together and then run by a committee. All animals and tools, and produce of the farm, were to be shared

Communists the new name for the Bolsheviks, adopted by Lenin in 1918

dictator a ruler whose power is not restricted by a constitution, laws or recognised opposition

dissident a person who disagrees with the government, often publicly

Duma the Russian parliament, established by Nicholas II after the 1905 revolution

kolkhoz a collective farm (*see* **collectivisation**)

kulak a rich peasant who often owned his own animals and land

Marxist a follower of the economic and political theory of Karl Marx (1818–83)

Menshevik a member of one of the groups formed after the split of the Social Democratic Party in 1903 (*see* **Bolshevik**). They believed that the Party should be a mass organisation which all workers could join and which would eventually take power

pogrom organised persecution of Jews

Politburo the executive and policy-making committee of the Communist Party in the USSR

proletariat the (industrial) working class. A term often used in Marxist theory

serf an unfree person, often bound to the land he works on and owned by the landowner

show trial the trial of a prominent politician or opponent of the government, organised to demonstrate the authority of those in power. Stalin established his control by a series of show trials in the 1930s

Socialist a supporter of the economic theory whereby the means of production are owned by the community collectively, usually through the state

Socialist Revolutionaries a political party formed in 1901. Its members believed in a general revolutionary movement which would unite all the people who were suffering under the Tsar

Soviet a workers' council; later a central part of the Soviet system of government at local, regional and national level

starets a holy man; literally an 'elder'

totalitarian a state in which every aspect of people's lives is controlled and monitored by those in power, e.g. in the USSR under Stalin and in Germany under Hitler. No opposition to the ruling power is allowed

Index